One Nation, One Standard

With warmest regards

Herma Badillo

HERMAN BADILLO

One Nation,
One Standard

An Ex-Liberal on
How Hispanics Can Succeed
Just Like Other Immigrant Groups

SENTINEL

SENTINEL

Published by the Penguin Group

Penguin Group (USA) Inc., 375 Hudson Street, New York, New York 10014, U.S.A. •
Penguin Group (Canada), 90 Eglinton Avenue East, Suite 700, Toronto, Ontario, Canada M4P
2Y3 (a division of Pearson Penguin Canada Inc.) • Penguin Books Ltd, 80 Strand, London
WC2R 0RL, England • Penguin Ireland, 25 St. Stephen's Green, Dublin 2, Ireland (a divi-
sion of Penguin Books Ltd) • Penguin Books Australia Ltd, 250 Camberwell Road,
Camberwell, Victoria 3124, Australia (a division of Pearson Australia Group Pty Ltd) •
Penguin Books India Pvt Ltd, 11 Community Centre, Panchsheel Park, New Delhi–110 017,
India • Penguin Books (NZ), Cnr Airborne and Rosedale Roads, Albany, Auckland 1310,
New Zealand (a division of Pearson New Zealand Ltd) • Penguin Books (South Africa) (Pty)
Ltd, 24 Sturdee Avenue, Rosebank, Johannesburg 2196, South Africa

Penguin Books Ltd, Registered Offices:
80 Strand, London WC2R 0RL, England

First published in 2006 by Sentinel,
a member of Penguin Group (USA) Inc.

1   3   5   7   9   10   8   6   4   2

PHOTOGRAPH CREDITS: Author's personal archive: insert pp. 1 (two photos), 7 (top), 8 (two);
courtesy of the White House: p. 6 (bottom); © Andy Marcus / www.fredmarcus.com: p. 7 (bottom).
All others courtesy of *El Diario/La Prensa*.

LIBRARY OF CONGRESS CATALOGING-IN-PUBLICATION DATA
Badillo Herman, 1929–
    One nation, one standard / Herman Badillo.
        p.   cm.
    Includes index.
    ISBN 978-1-59523-019-5
    1. Hispanic Americans—Social conditions.   2. Hispanic Americans—Cultural assimilation.
    3. Hispanic Americans—Education.   4. Hispanic Americans—Economic conditions.
    5. Hispanic American families.   6. Immigrants—United States—Social conditions.
    7. United States—Ethnic relations.   8. United States—Social policy.   9. Language policy—
    United States.   10. Badillo, Herman, 1929–   I. Title.
    E184.S75B332006
    305.868'073—dc22   2006050456

Printed in the United States of America
Set in American Garamond

To my wife, Gail,
my once-in-a-lifetime love

Foreword

by Rudolph W. Giuliani

I FIRST GOT TO KNOW Herman Badillo well early in the 1993 election cycle for New York City's top offices. I was running for mayor, and Herman was considering a bid for City Hall himself. Though he was a Democrat and I was a Republican, our ideas about what the city most needed at that critical time were similar—almost identical.

In the end, my team and I were able to persuade Herman to run for comptroller on a fusion ticket, with me in the top slot. I will always regret that Herman didn't win. And I will always be grateful to him for helping to put me over the top on Election Day.

Herman took a lot of flak from his Democratic friends for supporting a Republican. But, to paraphrase what Ronald Reagan once said of his own political journey, they left Herman; Herman didn't leave them. He watched—as I did—a party devoted to strength abroad and prosperity at home transform itself into a party of defeatism, excuses, and gloom. Throughout, Herman's beliefs never changed. He found himself increasingly out of step with his party and with many of lifelong friends and colleagues. But he found a new party, new purpose, and new friends. And I am proud to be one of them.

Herman's political journey can partly be explained by his passionate desire to see that every young kid in New York City—and every young kid America—can enjoy the same advantages that he had. It might seem strange to talk about the "advantages" of someone who came to this country desperately poor and speaking not a word of English, but that's not the way Herman sees it. To him, being able to live in the freest country in the world, in the greatest city on earth, and especially to be educated by what was once the best public education system in the nation, were unparalleled advantages. Herman watched with dismay as the system that served him and millions like him so well decayed into a bureaucratic monolith more concerned with protecting jobs than educating kids.

As a candidate and as mayor, I found Herman's advice on all subjects invaluable, but none more so than his counsel on education. It took a long time for Herman's ideas to break through the resistance, but his legacy is considerable. In New York, the dysfunctional Board of Education is finally gone and accountability is in. The City University of New York, or CUNY—which educated Herman superbly but failed more recent generations—has raised standards and improved graduation rates. I think Herman even deserves some of the credit for the federal No Child Left Behind Act. It was Herman who put raising standards at the center of the education debate.

Standards are important to Herman, and not just in education. He was the first to use what became my campaign slogan: "One City, One Standard." New York was then a divided city, by design. The political establishment and the interest groups wanted it that way because the divisions increased their power. But Herman saw that they weakened the city as a whole, setting people against one another and convincing them that the city's good things constituted a pie to be greedily divided rather than a garden to be carefully cultivated by all. Herman saw a better, brighter, truer vision because he had lived it and still lived it. He never wanted to be thought of simply as a Hispanic, or as an immigrant, or as someone from a poor background. His dignity demanded that he be judged as a man, that his accomplishments be taken seriously on the merits, and that he be rewarded or otherwise on the basis of what he has *done,* rather than who he was.

The greatest lesson of Herman Badillo's story is that the genius of American life—the upward ladder of opportunity that American freedom at its best provides—is better at solving most any problem than any government program. It's better for the poor, for workers, for the middle class, for small towns and great cities, and for the country as a whole. It is a lesson that America would do well to heed today.

Contents

Foreword by Rudolph W. Giuliani   *vii*

1. The Crisis We Face   *1*

2. Beyond the Mountains   *9*

3. The Five-Century Siesta   *35*

4. The Politics of Education   *49*

5. One Country, Two Languages   *57*

6. Social Promotion and Other Implements
   of Ignorance   *73*

7. The Harvard of the Poor   *109*

8. From Kennedy Democrat to Giuliani Republican   *139*

9. Toward a Unified Culture   *177*

10. The Hispanic Community in the United
    States and Latin America: The Next Fifty Years   *191*

11. One Nation, One Standard   *205*

    Acknowledgments   *215*

    Notes   *216*

    Index   *220*

1

The Crisis We Face

FEW AMERICANS REALIZE that the influx of foreign-born Hispanics to the United States since the Second World War is larger in relative size than the European migration here in the late nineteenth and early twentieth centuries.

The Hispanic march into the United States poses a crisis that America still has not fully faced. While we await a rational policy on this mass migration, these new immigrants are not assimilating and succeeding as previous arrivals have done. In many ways they keep falling behind. Of all measured ethnic groups, Hispanics have the highest rates of poverty and dropping out of high school, and the lowest proportions of politicians and millionaires.

How did Hispanics fall so far behind other immigrants? Why do they struggle to catch up, generation after generation after generation? Why can't they use the experiences of other ethnic groups to match their accomplishments? Or why don't Hispanics chart their own course—develop their own Operation Bootstrap—to pull even with everyone else?

This book offers a framework for addressing those issues, informed by lessons learned in my long career as a Hispanic public servant. I feel uniquely qualified to speak about these problems, because I played a part in causing some of them. As a member of Congress, for instance, I led efforts to establish bilingual voting and bilingual education programs. While well intentioned, these programs, especially the latter, backfired drastically because of the explosive combination of racial politics and the ingrained incompetence of our public-school systems. Meanwhile, although the pilot programs I developed in housing, employment, health, and education did achieve some successes, the national support that these programs require has varied between elusive and totally nonexistent.

These lessons have led me to conclude that government interventions, such as those I helped implement, cannot transport the Hispanic community to a better future. We must not delude ourselves into believing that government will provide Hispanics with adequate health care, employment, or housing for all—or even offer their children proper education. Instead we must understand the reasons for both the immigration and the under-achievement, so that Hispanics can be given the means to improve their own lives.

In the pages that follow, I try to impart that understanding. In the next chapter, I begin by telling the story of my own immigration to the United States and what I've learned since then about the cultural values that promote or prevent assimilation into the American mainstream. I discuss the excellent public education I received, the vision of progress I tried to advance during my decades of public service, and some of the stark realities of ethnic roles in American life. I then detail some of the key characteristics of immigrant groups that have successfully Americanized, and show how Hispanics have fallen short.

In chapter 3, I trace these shortcomings to the cultural legacy of Spain. Her colonial intentions in the Americas—to mine gold and to convert souls—bred stratified, quasi-feudal systems in her former colonies. The dead hands of this past—the stifling conditions created during a five-century political siesta—have not only caused the mass migration of Hispanics but have put them at a disadvantage when they get here. Among these conditions are a disregard for the rule of law, an indifference to participatory democracy (in the 2004 presidential election, 18 percent of Hispanics voted, compared with 39 percent of blacks and 51 percent of whites), and a lack of enthusiasm for education.

In chapter 4, I discuss the general elements of what I call the "politics of education." Education has always been the gateway to success in the United States. The Hispanic community, however, has been handicapped not only by its own attitudes toward learning but by homegrown bureaucratic incompetence. Instead of pulling them up the social ladder, America's failing public-school systems have pushed Hispanics down. Paralyzed by racially themed power struggles among teachers' unions, parents, politicians, and bureaucrats, our public schools have shunted Hispanics into low-intensity classes and asked too little of them, implicitly convinced of their inability to achieve. We have shut in Hispanic faces the gate that previous groups used to enter the American mainstream.

In chapter 5, I consider more specifically the failure of Hispanics to learn English. In 1973, during my second term in Congress, I sponsored legislation creating America's first bilingual-education programs in our nation's public schools. These programs aimed to provide non–English speakers the same educational opportunities that other students enjoyed. Yet although intended as a bridge to full English comprehension, bilingual education has become in practice a substitute for it. Because bilingualism has actually become monolingualism, it has hindered not only Hispanic progress in education but, more broadly, Hispanic assimilation into American life.

In chapter 6, I examine other educational practices that undermine Hispanic achievement. Social promotion, academic tracking, and the misuse of special-education classes are prevalent in (but not exclusive to) New York City, where I have battled politically against them. Social promotion, the most debilitating of these practices, means simply the "advancement" of students from grade to grade, not based on their ability to perform but in order to prevent the alleged sociological harm of being held back. Tracking, the streamlining of students into different levels of classes based on their academic ability, amounts in conjunction with this policy to de facto segregation. Special education, originally intended as a necessary aid to those students with severe disabilities, has meanwhile become little more than a dumping ground for any student who is in any way disruptive. Ethnic minorities, including Hispanics, make up the vast majority of those harmed by these policies. Because Hispanic students are too seldom held accountable for academic failure, they too often fail.

These failures have been especially spectacular in our public colleges and universities, as I show in chapter 7. A poignant lesson is provided here by the demise and revival of the City University of New York (CUNY), once known as "the Harvard of the Poor." After a 1969 student strike for minority access to education led to a policy of "open admissions," CUNY nosedived in three decades from one of America's top public universities into one of its worst, becoming little more than a holding pen for underprepared high-school students. As chairman of the board of trustees of the City University, I fought a long and difficult—but ultimately successful—battle to restore CUNY's once-high academic standards. We reimposed entrance requirements, and CUNY is now back on its way up. Most hearteningly, despite dire warnings that entrance requirements would "push out" blacks and Hispanics, their enrollment has actually *risen* since standards were reimposed.

In chapter 8, I recount in detail my political involvement with Mayor Rudolph Giuliani. A lifelong liberal Democrat, I had regretfully seen Democratic mayors demonstrate colossal incompetence, from Abe Beame's fiscal follies to David Dinkins's mishandling of the Crown Heights riots in 1991. But more than anything, what drew me to run with him and, later, to switch parties altogether was Giuliani's commitment to reforming public education and reducing crime—two issues affecting all New Yorkers, but especially Hispanics.

Though Giuliani and I campaigned side by side, the question of whether Hispanic and Anglo cultures can peacefully coexist is a more complicated one, as I discuss in chapter 9. Although the Hispanic community has established itself in America in large part by retaining its separate identity, this very sense of difference has played no small role in ensuring that Hispanics remain politically, culturally, and economically marginalized. Bilingualism and multiculturalist identity politics have produced an ingrained resistance to acculturation. This resistance must be overcome if Hispanics are to enter the American mainstream. Until then, Hispanics (and U.S. policy makers) must understand that the failure to enter the mainstream is due more to self-segregation within the Hispanic community than to discrimination against Hispanics from without.

In chapter 10, I chart a course for Hispanic achievement in the next half century. Stemming the flow of illegal immigration would lessen the American Hispanic community's problems but would require addressing the root cause of the exodus. Can the Latin American countries be economically transformed by foreign encouragement and guidance? Education and crime-control programs created by the Manhattan Institute's Latin American Initiative and the Caribbean Basin Initiative implemented by President Ronald Reagan but, alas, applied only in Grenada should serve as models for U.S. development efforts in Latin America. Yet these efforts must be tempered by realism, not only about the effects of development aid in other parts of the world but about the legacies of the long cultural sleep from which the Hispanic world is only now beginning to awaken.

In my final chapter, I lay out what I believe are the keys to the assimilation of the old and the new immigrants—the principles that have made and will keep us one nation, under one standard.

Although the problems confronting Hispanics are daunting and although solving them will require patience and political will, one thing is clear. American Hispanics need, first and foremost, to envision and adopt a completely new culture of self-improvement. Certainly this can be done, and the time to start is now. The opportunities for advancement that existed for yesterday's European immigrants still exist today. Hispanics must expend the considerable energy necessary to achieve, as other immigrant groups have done. Above all they must learn that the true solutions to their problems lie not with government but within themselves.

2

Beyond the Mountains

WHEN I EMIGRATED from Puerto Rico to the United States, in April of 1941, I was an eleven-year-old orphan who spoke little English. I came from Caguas, a small town that had been devastated by an epidemic of tuberculosis. My father, a schoolteacher, died when I was a year old, my mother when I was five, both of tuberculosis.

I went to live with my aunt Aurelia and her two children. We were then very poor: This was during the Depression, which was actually worse in Puerto Rico than it was in the United States. I would go hungry for days—attending school, coming back to the house, and finding nothing to eat, over and over.

When I was about six or seven years old, my two cousins would go begging in the town square for money and come back with some money. They would do this regularly, and my aunt used the money to buy food. But I, out of pride and stubbornness, refused to eat the food, because I was against begging. They actually worried that I was going to starve to death. Aunt Aurelia addressed my refusal to eat by finding me a job cleaning the floor of a wealthy family's apartment in exchange for food. I never knew how well I performed my duties, but this plan satisfied my personal sense of morality.

Two other activities complemented my life. One was my love of the mountains and the outdoors. As soon as I could, probably at age seven, I climbed to the top of the mountain in front of my house and peered over to the other side. Green peaks stretched on and on forever. That thrilled me. I spent many weekends hiking in the mountains and visiting relatives on foot in Cidra and Cayey, two towns that were several miles away. I also wandered through the sugarcane fields and loved to chew the cane as I traveled.

The second activity, which I never skipped, was Sunday school in Caguas's only Protestant church. Every Sunday I awoke early, got dressed, grabbed my Bible, and walked alone approximately a mile to the local Baptist church. It was a tiny place a few blocks from the town square. I went alone because I was the only Protestant in my family and, apparently, the only Protestant in our neighborhood.

In fact, during my youth there were few Protestants in Caguas or anywhere else in Puerto Rico. The island had belonged to Spain until 1898, and Spain was Catholic. Years later, when I was already a lawyer and returned to Aquadilla, my family's hometown, I learned that the Badillo family had been among the founding families of Puerto Rico's Protestant movement. The name of Antonio Badillo (1827–1889) appears in local history books as a founder of a group called "the Biblicals" that practiced Protestantism, something apparently illegal back then. Someone once saw the word "Protestant" on my ancestor's tombstone and said, "Badillos are troublemakers, even when dead."

For whatever reason, a substantial number of Badillos have been Protestant ministers or lawyers. The legend was that the ministers practiced Protestantism, whereupon the lawyers sprang them from jail.

I don't remember being told to do so as a child, but somebody, probably my dying mother, must have impressed upon me that I had to attend the Protestant church, even if I had to go alone. I never missed a Sunday morning there.

It's quite possible, given all these tragedies and enormous setbacks, that I might have spent the rest of my life in Puerto Rico, trying to rebuild what bad luck had destroyed, had my aunt not finally accumulated enough money to immigrate, along with me and one of her children, to the United States.

My first years in America were not exactly settled. Soon after landing in Manhattan, I was sent off to Chicago and then to Burbank, California, to live with my uncle Tomás. Unlike many other members of my extended American family, Tomás had already begun to live the American dream—he had a high-paying job with Lockheed Martin. It was while living with Tomás in Burbank that I learned English—the first step on my road to becoming a real American.

Uncle Tomás worked at the Lockheed plant in that Los Angeles suburb. He apparently had a very good job. He and his wife owned a one-family home in a residential neighborhood where the houses all had beautiful front and back lawns. My uncle was the only Puerto Rican or Hispanic in the community. His wife, Janice, was an Irishwoman who spoke no Spanish. They had two very small children.

It was clear to me that neither Uncle Tomás nor Aunt Janice was particularly happy to have me with them, because they paid me very little attention, Janice, in particular, showed by her manner that I was not a responsibility she cared to assume. It was the middle of the academic year, but nobody said anything to me about enrolling in school. After a couple of weeks, I followed some kids about my age to Burbank Junior High School, about a mile away, and enrolled myself in the school.

About three weeks later, my uncle said Aunt Janice wondered what I did during the day, because I left early in the morning and returned in the afternoon. I told them I was going to school. He looked stunned and said I could not speak English. I told him I had enrolled myself and was learning the language.

I was making a very concerted effort to learn to speak English. I used to study whenever and wherever I could. I remember sitting in the school library one day, trying to learn how to pronounce quietly a particularly difficult word. Suddenly I felt my tongue snap. "Oh, my God," I thought. "I tried so hard that I broke my tongue." I erupted in a sweat and was terrified to open my mouth for fear that my tongue would fall out. For the longest time, I was too frightened to move. Then, gradually, I moved the tip of my tongue against my teeth and, to my immense relief, concluded that it was still intact and attached to my mouth. I couldn't have been happier, but for a long time I avoided difficult words.

One of the strangest things that happened to me— considering that I was only just barely fluent in English—was that I got involved with the student government and somehow got myself elected class president. This was potentially a huge embarrassment: I was supposed to lead the class in the national anthem and the Pledge of Allegiance. I knew neither. Fortunately, I eventually figured them out.

After almost two years in California, I was sent back to Manhattan, just in time to enroll in junior high school there.

In 1944, I graduated from junior high and was assigned to

Haaren High School, at Tenth Avenue and Fifty-ninth Street. At Haaren I was enrolled in the vocational program, which meant studying airplane mechanics. I took courses in making blueprints, mechanical drawing, and drafting. I learned how to take apart and put together again internal combustion engines, and I made many model airplanes. All of this I felt competent to do, but I found it rather boring. It was assumed that because of my background, I would finish high school with a mechanic's degree and then go off and get a job repairing military or commercial aircraft.

I happened upon a copy of the school newspaper, and soon joined its staff. I began as its inquiring photographer, asking students topical questions and reporting their answers. But before long, I began writing feature stories.[1] I interviewed Peggy Lee, who had just embarked upon her singing career. Readers seemed impressed with my profile.

One day another student who wrote for the newspaper asked me, "Are you a student in this school? How come we don't see you in any of our classes?"

"Of course I am," I replied. "I'm taking airplane mechanics."

"What are you doing that for?" he asked. "That's for blacks and Puerto Ricans."

"Well," I answered, "I *am* Puerto Rican."

"You don't understand," he said. "You're obviously very bright, even though you have a strong Spanish accent, but you're enrolled in a vocational course. You should be with us in the academic courses, because you should go to college."

"I don't have any money for college," I said. "In fact, I'm working now as a short-order cook at the Automat."

"It doesn't matter," my friend said. "City College is free, and you'll get in if you have an academic diploma."

I took his advice and switched from vocational study to the school's college-oriented academic path. This conversation with my friend at the school newspaper's office was a turning point in my life.[2] Suddenly I realized I could look beyond the mountains.[3]

After this stroke of good luck, I would go on to major in business and accounting at CUNY and to take a law degree from Brooklyn Law School. The public-education system in this country, whatever its problems now, did work well, even for minorities, when I was young.

But one thing was apparent to me in the middle of this strange new world. Almost from the first day I arrived in New York, it was clear to me that in the United States you are judged by the color of your skin. If you are white, you are a member of the majority, and while there may be some limited discrimination because you may belong to a particular ethnic group (of Irish, Italian, or Jewish stock, for example), you remain a European and therefore part of the accepted culture. If you are black, you are not part of the majority culture, and you are regarded as somehow inferior to the majority and thus become part of a minority subculture. The division into majority and minority is very rigid in this country; if even a small portion of your ancestry is African-American, you are regarded as black and as a part of the minority or inferior culture. I believe this is still true today.

This division creates a special problem for us in the Puerto Rican and Hispanic community. Puerto Ricans and Hispanics are not a race. Just like others in the Western Hemisphere, Puerto Ricans and Hispanics are European, African-American, Native American, Asian, or a combination of any of these groups. The difference is that we do not draw a rigid line in Latin American culture: We do not divide ourselves into a majority culture and a minority culture. I have never heard a Puerto Rican refer to himself or herself as a white Puerto Rican, a black Puerto Rican, or a hyphenated Puerto Rican of any kind. We just don't think in those terms. While we obviously recognize that some are white, some are black, and some are mixed, we think of ourselves as Puerto Ricans. Period. Puerto Rican society does not recognize majority or minority cultures. This is not to say that there is no individual discrimination on the part of some people, but simply that it is not a culturally accepted standard.

The lack of rigidity on the issue of skin color leads to more natural relationships among ourselves. None of us would think it strange to see a black Puerto Rican dancing with a white

Puerto Rican, for example. Indeed, in the Puerto Rican and Latin American dance halls in New York City, people of all shades dance and sit together at dinner tables and enjoy themselves in a relaxed atmosphere that does not exist in many places outside the Latino community.

I have discussed elsewhere the historical reasons why the two societies have developed into such different cultures, but such an important issue bears repeating. I believe that the main reason for this distinction was the influence of religion, which was the primary institution in both societies at their inception in the Western Hemisphere. In Puerto Rico and Latin America, the Catholic Church was the most important institution, probably even more important than the state itself. For example, every town and city in Puerto Rico has a town square called the plaza. My hometown, Caguas, is typical. On one side of the plaza is City Hall, the official seat of power of the government. On the other side of the plaza is the Catholic church. The townspeople believed that if you wanted anything done, you should clear it with the church before you consulted City Hall.

When I was a child, the Catholic Church was considered the most important institution in town. The church's influence had significant repercussions in establishing the island's cultural institutions. There is only one Catholic Church, and its sacraments are binding on all Catholics. Catholicism was the only recognized religion in Puerto Rico until the late nineteenth century; thus, during the existence of slavery in Puerto Rico, the masters and the slaves attended the same Catholic church and were bound by the same sacraments. If two slaves were married in the church, their bonds of holy matrimony had to be recognized by the masters. If the married couple had children who were baptized in the same church, the children's legitimacy had to be recognized. In effect, masters and slaves were equal in the eyes of Rome.

In the United States, the predominant religious institution was Protestantism, with its many underlying denominations. The Protestant churches developed into two separate institutions: the white and the black, with the African Methodist and the Episcopal (AME) being among the most prominent of the black churches. Slaves were not allowed to belong to the same church as their master, and the masters did not consider the black church equal to the white church; if slaves were married in the black church, their marriages were not recognized by the white church, nor were the children of such marriages considered legitimate.

It followed that there would be two separate school systems, two separate groups of private institutions, two separate sets of public facilities. In short, two societies. Even when slavery was abolished, the two societies remained in place. Not until the Civil Rights Act of 1964 was segregation officially abolished. This landmark legislation was only possible because of the efforts of the Reverend Dr. Martin Luther King Jr., and because President Lyndon B. Johnson was at the height of his popularity and was able to push it through Congress. Nevertheless, segregation is still a reality in many parts of this country. For example, on the Upper East Side, you seldom see African-Americans in any significant numbers. However, when you travel the subway system, you see that more than three quarters of the people are black or Latino. A visitor would have to conclude that there are still two separate societies.

In Puerto Rico, because of the influence of the Catholic Church, there were never two separate school systems, two separate groups of private institutions, two separate sets of public facilities, or two separate societies. Since the abolition of slavery there, only one society has existed. This does not mean that there has been no individual discrimination, but because there has been no *institutional* discrimination, relations among the races have never been as strained in Puerto Rico as they are in this country.

It really is impossible to detail the difference in attitudes because I am talking about emotions that cannot be explained logically. Those of us who were born in Puerto Rico and lived in that Latin culture during our early years simply have a totally different perception of skin color from the perceptions that exist here. That is why I consider New York a divided city.

Certainly, the divisions between blacks and Puerto Ricans

could not be overlooked at the junior high school I attended after I returned from California. Manhattanville Junior High School was about equally divided between African-Americans and Puerto Ricans. It was not a good school in terms of educational quality. I found it easy to get good grades, although there was little discipline in the classroom and none outside on the streets.

I was about fourteen years old at this time and was growing very rapidly, eventually reaching a height of six feet, one inch. I was very athletic, thanks to my mountain climbing in California, and I kept in great shape by doing fifty push-ups every day, walking on my hands, and performing an assortment of calisthenics.

I soon learned that good looks and light skin were not assets for a Puerto Rican in my neighborhood. One time I was walking with a beautiful Puerto Rican girl on my arm up Broadway, and was punched in the face by a group of blacks who approached from the opposite direction. On another occasion, I was playing basketball with some black kids in the school gym and, in the middle of a clash, was staggered by a nasty punch in the mouth. After that, I learned to be cautious and take notice of the people around me.

My saddest experience involved an African-American student who sat next to me in some of my classes. His name was Keith, and he took boxing lessons. We became good friends because we were both athletes. This became very clear when a teacher tested our class's reaction time by measuring how quickly we could stop a bell from ringing once instructed to do so. Keith and I both reacted as quickly as top athletes—far better than anyone else in our class.

Keith and I occupied adjoining seats in a double row in the middle of the classroom. We sat about six inches apart. That semester I noticed that Keith kept looking at me, but I thought nothing of it. One day, I had my right arm resting on my desktop. Keith, who sat to my right, put his left arm on my arm and said, "Gee, what beautiful white skin." I was stunned, for it had never occurred to me to think of Keith as black, and I did not know what to say to him. But, looking at him, I felt an overwhelming sadness because I realized he truly believed that his skin color would prevent him from having the same opportunities in life that I would have. I reached out and touched his arm to reassure him that our different skin colors were not important to me.

I have often thought about this incident, because it showed me that America's rigid racism—which I acknowledge is not politically correct to discuss, but which is still evident to us who come from a different culture—damages individuals. It has made me determined to avoid the pitfalls of racial polarization—not just for myself, but for the Puerto Rican and Hispanic community to which I belong. I have come to believe that the most important contribution we Latin Americans can make to America is to avoid racial labels, to refuse to divide ourselves along color lines, and to stay united as a group so we may show the larger society that it is possible to relate to one another without being separated by the wall of racism.

In the years following my graduation from Brooklyn Law School, I hung out a shingle and specialized in tax law. Additionally, being fluent in Spanish, I was often called on to do pro bono work for non-English-speaking clients, as there was a real shortage of attorneys and judges who spoke Spanish in New York in the early 1950s. I began to see firsthand the many issues faced by the Hispanic community in New York, and my frustration in trying to help them on a case-by-case basis led me to think of a career in politics, where I could address the basic social problems of New York's Hispanics and the rest of New York's disadvantaged people.

My first real political effort was a breakout registration campaign, in 1960, on behalf of John F. Kennedy. I managed to loosen the old-line Democratic stranglehold in East Harlem by registering hundreds of Hispanics. I even won a landmark case against the New York City Board of Elections, proving that fourteen Puerto Ricans had been denied the right to register to vote after waiting in line for hours. From then on I became a fixture in city politics, serving as an adviser and official for several mayors. I was appointed commissioner of housing relocation by Mayor Robert F. Wagner Jr. in 1962 and became the first Hispanic full commissioner in New York City history. I was elected Bronx borough president in 1965 and became the first-ever Hispanic borough president. As borough president I watched the South Bronx burn when Mayor John Lindsay ignored my advice on how to save it. After my own failed bid for the mayor's office in 1969, I was elected as the first Puerto Rican congressman in the history of the nation in 1970. I resigned from Congress in 1978 to become deputy mayor under the controversial Ed Koch, in charge of education and of rebuilding the South Bronx. I watched David Dinkins make a complete mess of his response to the riots in Crown Heights—also after ignoring my advice on how to end the racial tensions that ignited the riots. In short, over the course of my career, I watched New York in its long, slow decline from America's greatest metropolis to a city seemingly destined for failure, a descent that bottomed out in the late 1980s, shortly before I was appointed a trustee of CUNY by Mario Cuomo in 1990. And after forty years as a liberal Democrat, I'd had enough. I made a big decision: to run on the same ticket as the ex-prosecutor Rudolph Giuliani (who would appoint me, eight years later, to the task force he organized to overhaul the City University), in the hope of changing New York for the better. Eventually I would even become a Republican: Liberal politicians had simply run out of answers.

Working with Giuliani made a great deal of sense. We shared ideas about improving life in New York and about the need to hold people accountable for their own actions. Despite all the controversy surrounding Giuliani, I have to give him a lot of credit for dramatically reversing New York's long and painful fall. His administration had a deeply personal effect on me. I served both on the task force he organized to overhaul the City University of New York, my alma mater, and as chairman of CUNY's board of trustees during its worst years, and I fought to restore its former glory. This fight only made me believe more strongly that education is the most important tool for any immigrant trying to make himself at home in America.

As a resident of New York City, I've watched dozens of immigrant groups as they adjusted to life in America—from Puerto Ricans to the Vietnamese. Each of those groups underwent similar trials and tribulations; all of them had the same hurdles of poverty and discrimination to overcome. But their responses to these challenges, I saw, were as different as their countries of origin. Some of them flourished; some did not. The question of why some immigrants made it and some didn't has troubled politicians and sociologists in America for more than a century. This is a difficult question to answer, especially now, when the culture of political correctness dismisses any attempt at pattern recognition as "generalization" and "stereotyping."

But I am a New Yorker. Five decades spent in the rough-and-tumble political life of America's largest and most troubled city have a way of making a person blunt and plainspoken. If we talk about the vibrant mosaic of ethnic life in America and in New York, how can we not say openly that different ethnic groups, different cultures, have completely different values? There may be a lot of underlying common beliefs—a belief, for example, in the basic right to life, liberty, and the pursuit of happiness (the recent demonstrations by Hispanic immigrants prove how basic these common beliefs are). But each ethnic group has inherited a cultural identity from ancestors and brought it to this country. Asian-Americans place a very high value on the importance of education. Italian-Americans value community and tradition. Hispanics are free from the racialist attitudes that so many other Americans have.

But every immigrant group's cultural values can hurt them as well as help them. My battle for expanded voting rights for minorities—and the long-term results of my victory—illustrates these cultural values and the sometimes negative effect that these values can have on the lives of immigrants.

When the original Voting Rights Act came up for debate, in 1965, I called for the elimination of voting-related literacy tests. At that time I was still New York's commissioner of housing re-location and was the city's highest Hispanic appointed official. I argued that New York was the only northern state with a literacy test in its constitution, originally enacted to discriminate against Italian immigrants. In the 1960s, however, those in power used it to prevent Puerto Ricans and blacks from voting.

We failed to get Congress to abolish the literacy test, but an amendment to the Voting Rights Act was passed that exempted Puerto Ricans from it if they showed that they had completed at least the sixth grade in Puerto Rico, part of the American commonwealth. In 1975, as a U.S. House Judiciary Committee member, I worked with other colleagues to amend that schooling requirement and to eliminate the literacy test entirely from all states. In this we finally were victorious. We established beyond any doubt that literacy tests discriminated not only against blacks in the South and Puerto Ricans in New York but also against Mexicans in the entire American Southwest. Today the New York Board of Elections and others around the country provide for citizens to vote in Spanish and many other languages. The registration process also has been simplified so that people now can register to vote at any time during the year, by mail, and even at the polls on Election Day. Creating obstacles to registration and voting is still attempted by unscrupulous political leaders, but they are illegal and subject to prosecution. The Voting Rights Act is largely responsible for the huge increase in elected Latino leaders over the last forty years.

Yet there are a few important questions that no one has answered. Hispanics in America have enjoyed high levels of political influence in the past four decades. Why have they failed to adapt themselves to American life in the way that other immigrant groups have done? They've confronted the same hurdles: discrimination and a system that paid lip service to equality but in fact disenfranchised immigrants. They overcame those obstacles—at least at first. But why so much difference in progress between Hispanics and other immigrant groups? Why did voting reform and the upswing in the number of Hispanics elected to public office do so little, economically and socially, for American Hispanics? The problem with asking these questions is that no one wants to hear the answers. But, as I said, fifty years of political life in Manhattan and the Bronx have cured me of shyness.

Now for the hard part. The primary determinant of any immigrant group's success or failure in America is its attitude toward education. American Jews and Asian immigrants have succeeded because both of those cultures place an enormously high value on intellect, educational diligence, and hard work.

This becomes obvious if one considers the astounding fact that Americans of Asian heritage constitute only 4 percent of the U.S. population but 20 percent of Ivy League students, or if one reads the following, from UCLA professor Min Zhou:

Existing research on the new second generation has repeatedly shown that high school students of Asian origin outperform non-Hispanic white students who, in turn, outperform black and Hispanic students by a significantly large margin, even amongst those of relatively modest socioeconomic backgrounds. More strikingly, even the Hmong, who came from a preliterate peasant background, and the more recently arrived Cambodians outperformed all native-born American students attending the same school. Asian-Americans also . . . attend college at a rate significantly higher than that of whites and other racial minority groups.[4]

The children of the Asian community, both immigrants and native-born, are achieving extraordinary educational success in America's primary and secondary schools and then shining even more brightly in college. They have not been deterred by discrimination, poverty, language difficulties, ghettoization, or any of the factors that supporters of the culture of dependency claim as excuses for a lack of progress among Hispanics. The Asian community sets the pace for educational achievement and does so admirably.

The spectacular success of Asian children is evident even in an otherwise dysfunctional school system such as New York City's. The huge high-school dropout rate for black and Latino children does not apply to Asian kids. On the contrary, Gotham's elite high schools—such as Stuyvesant High School and Bronx High School of Science—have substantial Asian populations.

Since the public-school system has lacked standards for many decades, the explanation for Asian-descended students' excellent scores on standardized tests is the persistence of Asian parents in demanding diligent and serious academic effort from their children.

Dr. Soo Kim Abboud and Jane Kim are sisters, the children of Korean immigrants. Their parents came to the United States with two hundred dollars in their pockets. In 2006 the Kim sisters wrote a book called *Top of the Class: How Asian Parents Raise High Achievers—and How You Can Too.*[5] Every Hispanic parent in America should read this book. It unveils the "secrets" of success in the Asian community today. These include:

- instilling a love and need for learning and education
- developing a sense of family pride and loyalty
- promoting respect and desire for delayed gratification and sacrifice
- defining clearly your child's role as a student
- cultivating a respect for elders and for persons in positions of authority
- playing an active role in your child's education
- determining and developing your child's individual talents
- teaching your child to value academic success over social status or popularity
- helping your child view America as a land of opportunity

These ideas are so simple and straightforward that they hardly deserve to be called secrets. But there is no comparable culture among American Hispanics. As a community, Hispanics have simply failed to recognize the overriding importance of education. In 2005, Hispanics dropped out of high school at a rate of over 50 percent. Equally tragic is the fact that millions in the Hispanic community consider a high-school diploma a sign of accomplishment all by itself. College, in other words, is far from an automatic goal in a vast majority of Hispanic homes.

Indeed, the concept of planning for a college education from the time a baby is born is an uncommon ambition, even within Hispanic families that have been in America for three generations or more. In some families and in some neighborhoods, my own included, relatives and friends look derisively at those who love books. When I attended City College and lived in West Harlem, I was the only resident in my apartment building who owned a typewriter and stayed up late doing homework. My relatives and friends did not encourage me to remain in school. They considered my interest in books an eccentricity. I don't bring these things up to complain, but because they clearly show the low status of education within the Hispanic community.

My wife's sister has three children in Connecticut. By the time they were three years old, they were operating computers. Now, later in childhood, they read roughly twenty-five books a year. Upper-middle-class white children, when they enter the first grade, have already received the equivalent of twenty-five hundred hours of public-school instruction. Average kids in the South Bronx or Harlem or East Harlem, when they go into the first grade have had, if they're lucky, a hundred hours of instruction.

When I was housing relocation commissioner, I used to visit many Hispanic homes. In the vast majority of them, there was not a single book to be found. In many cases there was not even a newspaper. The only thing you could be sure to find was a television. It's natural enough: If the adults don't read in a family, why expect the children to read? This simply has to change.

Accepting the responsibility for changing this state of affairs means making sure that children must know they are accountable to their entire extended family for their scholastic performance. It means making sure that the adults in their life will question and scrutinize the children's accomplishments and behavior at all times. Accepting this responsibility means that the adults in every family must consider the school a part of the home. They must visit it, must know its principal and teachers, the counselors, its structure, and the child's relationship to the rest of the student body. The whole Hispanic community needs a total attitude adjustment regarding the importance of education. It needs a new mantra: *Educating our community is too important to leave to the educators.* Only this change in attitude will carry Hispanics into the American mainstream.

I am not suggesting that Hispanics suffer from some kind of genetic inferiority that limits their mental powers, or that Asian-Americans or American Jews possess some mysterious genetic advantage. I am simply making an observation, which I have drawn from my own experience and from the years I've spent thinking about how to solve the problems of the Hispanic community in America: Hispanics, as a culture, *do* place less stress on the importance of education than do other, more economically and socially successful immigrant groups.

The problem of this underemphasis is a product not of genetics but of cultural values. Its causes, and remedies, can be found in the history that shaped Hispanic culture, here and in Central and South America. The members of every immigrant group carry legacies from its original culture with them into their new life in America, and Hispanics are no exception. But "Hispanic" itself is a broad, all-purpose category, containing dozens of different cultures from different nations. Which leaves us with another hard question: Where does Hispanic culture come from?

One answer should come immediately to mind. Despite the great differences among the indigenous cultures in Central and South America that have contributed to the formation of American Hispanic life, they do have, with only a few exceptions, one major historical event in common: Spain colonized them, at some point. For good or ill—and there is a lot of ill—that colonization in large part is where Hispanic culture comes from. That is where any understanding of Hispanic culture in America must begin.

3

The Five-Century Siesta

IN THE TURBULENT century after Columbus discovered the Americas, Spain conquered the Caribbean, all of Central and South America except Brazil, and vast areas of North America, including what are now the states of Florida, Texas, and California. The political legacy that American Hispanics inherited from this conquest, and from the subsequent centuries of colonial government, remains one of the most important factors in modern Hispanic life. Though it is rarely acknowledged in this era of political correctness, in Latin American political and economic development, the years from 1500 to the present amount to what can only be called a five-century siesta.

When Columbus returned from his first voyage, he offered the Spanish crown a gift of unbelievable proportions: vast, unexplored, distant lands. But thanks to a general domestic tranquillity (unlike in England, where the bloody War of the Roses had just concluded with the ascension to the throne of Henry VII), there was little interest among Spanish families in packing their bags and sailing to the New World. However, two groups of Spaniards did itch to reach the Western Hemisphere. One was the hidalgos, the soldiers who had recently conquered and evicted the Moors after eight centuries of war. Later known as conquistadores, these warriors were skilled fighters, and they expected to be paid in gold or silver. However, they eventually accepted grants of land in the New World as the spoils of war. The other group of Spaniards who saw the New World as an opportunity was the Catholic priesthood. The priests considered Indians potential converts to Catholicism who could become good Christians.

The conquistadores defeated the Indians' leaders, but they did not massacre the Indians—they simply set up a new political structure in which they ruled over vassal towns governed in turn by native-run councils, a structure that remained in effect for more than three hundred years. This system, of course, coupled with the priests' vigorous efforts at proselytizing, encouraged active intermingling between Spaniards and Indians, which generated mestizo communities under Spanish rule.

Racial mixing was not limited to Amerindians and whites.

When slaves were brought from Africa, they, too, were regarded as potential converts, and there also was much racial mixing between whites and blacks. Their offspring were called mulattoes or *morenos*. Indeed, all kinds of racial combinations became recognized in Latin America, thus obviating the rigid black-and-white separation line that developed in the United States and still constitutes one of the country's most serious problems.

But this nonracialist attitude, which I believe is the Hispanic community's most outstanding contribution, does not address the community's internal problems. These problems and their solutions lie deeper in Hispanic political and social legacy, another inheritance from Spain.

Imperial Spain did nothing to encourage a democratic system of government or to establish a meaningful New World educational system. Nor was it interested in politically colonizing Latin America as much as it wanted to mine its precious metals and exploit its natural resources. The Spanish conquest of Latin America was a tug-of-war between the conquistadores and the Indians over control of silver and gold. The Spanish crown, along with that of Portugal, controlled the political and economic structure totally and had no interest in either creating democratic institutions or educating the masses. During the initial period of colonization, Spain's principal goal was to seize as much silver and gold as possible. By 1600, the colonies had produced more than 2 billion pesos' worth, three times the total European supply before Columbus's first voyage, according to Juan Gonzalez in his valuable book *Harvest of Empire*.[1]

As time went on, *encomiendas,* grants of land and people to the conquistadores, became the primary institution in New Spain. As Elizabeth de Lima-Dantas and her colleagues wrote for the Library of Congress in 1985:

> The Spanish government established a series of rights and obligations between the *encomendero* (grantee) and the people under his care. The indigenous people were required to provide tribute and free labor to the *encomendero,* who was responsible for their welfare, their assimilation into Spanish culture, and their Christianization. Political and social stratification among the *encomenderos* was easily achieved by the simple fact that there were communities of different sizes. The larger the grant, the larger the amount of tribute and labor available, and thus the greater the potential wealth and prestige of assignment. In reality, the native population was accustomed to a similar organization of tributary towns under the Aztec. In time, the *encomenderos* became the New World version of Spanish feudal lords.[2]

This is the Spanish crown's legacy to the New World—the imposition of a new feudalism, which the rest of Europe had recently outgrown.

When Napoleon conquered Spain in 1808, his forces routed the Spanish and imprisoned Ferdinand VII. Napoleon installed his brother Joseph as king of Spain, and Joseph sought to obtain control of the colonies in the New World. The colonies refused to accept France's leadership. From this conflict arose the spring tide of Latin nations: Venezuela and Paraguay won independence in 1811; Argentina in 1816; Colombia in 1819; Central America, the Dominican Republic, and Mexico in 1821; Chile and Peru in 1824; Bolivia and Uruguay in 1825. Only Cuba and Puerto Rico remained in the Spanish Empire, which had regained its monarchy after Napoleon's defeat.

Unfortunately, these triumphant revolutions did not yield any significant changes in the social structure of Latin America. A new era, the era of the caudillo, descended and has remained in place ever since. A series of caudillos, most of whom came from the military, rose to power: Juan Manuel de Rosas ruled much of Argentina for twenty-one years in the mid-nineteenth century; Rafael Carrera ruled for eighteen years in Guatemala. Porfirio Díaz ran Mexico nonstop from 1884 to 1911; General Getulio Vargas controlled Brazil from 1930 to 1945. More recent examples? Perón in Argentina, Castro in Cuba, Balaguer in the Dominican Republic, Somoza in Nicaragua, Torrijos in Panama, Pinochet in Chile, Chávez in Venezuela, Morales in Bolivia. Need I name any more names?

In February 2005, a former public official from Bolivia

visited me in New York. He told me that Bolivia's recently elected president was rewriting his country's entire constitution. Sadly, neither my visitor nor his countrymen thought there was anything improper in this proposal. In no country in Latin America today is there a permanent constitution that recognizes the rights of individual citizens and cannot be nullified by the president and the legislature.

It is not hard to see the fruits of this centuries-long absence of real, participatory democracy. Good public education is often one of the first casualties of a breakdown in social order. Or, indeed, of a nation's failure to establish stable sociopolitical institutions. In any serious survey of modern Latin American life, one of the features most notable to U.S. eyes is the distressingly low level of educational achievement among Latin Americans in their own countries:

Country	Years of Compulsory Education	Average Years of Education Completed
Argentina	9	8.8
Bolivia	8	5.6
Brazil	8	4.9
Chile	12	10.1
Colombia	10	11
Costa Rica	10	6
Ecuador	10	6.4
El Salvador	9	5.2
Guatemala	11	3.5
Haiti	6	2.8

Country	Years of Compulsory Education	Average Years of Education Completed
Mexico	10	7.2
Nicaragua	6	4.6
Peru	11	8.9
Uruguay	10	7.6
Venezuela	7	6.6
United States	12	12

Most discouraging of all is this April 2004 United Nations poll of nearly twenty thousand people in eighteen Latin American countries:

- Just 43 percent of Latin Americans fully support democracy, while 30.5 percent express ambivalence about it and 26.5 percent hold nondemocratic views.
- More than half of all Latin Americans, 54.7 percent, say they would support an "authoritarian regime over democratic government" if authoritarianism would "resolve" their economic problems.
- "I believe in an authoritarian government, if it works," said Daniel Vargas, twenty-four, a university student from Ilave, Peru. "They do this in other countries and it works. Look at Cuba, that works. Look at Pinochet in Chile, that worked."
- Since 2000, four elected presidents in the eighteen countries studied were forced to quit before the end of their terms following steep drops in public support.

- The first generation of Latin Americans to grow up in "functioning democracies" has experienced virtually no per capita income growth in a context of world-record disparities in the distribution of national income.

- In 2003, 224 million Latin Americans had incomes below the poverty line (out of a total regional population of 534 million).

- Of the political leaders the UN pollsters interviewed, 59 percent said political parties are failing to fulfill their necessary roles.

This, then, is the legacy that the five-century siesta—the three hundred years of colonial rule and the subsequent two hundred years of authoritarian leadership—has bestowed upon the people of Latin America.

In the middle of the twentieth century, shortly after the end of the Second World War, Latin Americans in significant numbers came to the conclusion that this tragic legacy could not be overcome in their own countries. Possibly the war itself made them conscious of how advanced in economic and technological development the United States was, compared to Latin America. For whatever reason, the poor of the Caribbean and mainland Central America decided that economic conditions were not going to improve in their own countries and, as the Europeans had done a century earlier, decided to look to the United

States as the land of opportunity. First came the Puerto Ricans, followed by Mexicans, Dominicans, Cubans, and then citizens of mainland Central and Latin American nations. The 2000 U.S. census showed that more than one person in eight in the United States is of Hispanic origin. It also revealed that Hispanics represent 27.5 percent of the U.S. population below the age of seventeen, while Anglos account for 23.5 percent in the same age group. (Keep in mind also that the Hispanic population is undercounted, due to the significant numbers of undocumented immigrants.)

Hispanics are now America's largest minority. At 42 million in 2006, they constitute 14.2 percent of the total U.S. population, not including Puerto Rico's 4 million residents. In the next fifty years, their numbers are projected to grow to over 102 million—equal to 24 percent of America's population—thanks to natural birth rates and continued immigration, both legal and illegal. Thus we can undoubtedly expect their influence to grow in every aspect of American life.

Most dramatically, there is an imminent explosion in the number of eligible voters, which could prove decisive in national politics and in the largest states of the union. Already in 2004 there were thirteen states where people of Hispanic origin constituted more than 10 percent of the population. These were: California (34.7 percent), New York (16.0 percent), Texas (34.6 percent), Florida (19.0 percent), New Jersey (14.9 percent), Illinois (14.0

percent), New Mexico (43.3 percent), Arizona (28.0 percent), Nevada (22.8 percent), Colorado (19.1 percent), Connecticut (10.6 percent), Utah (10.6 percent), Rhode Island (10.3 percent).

The migration continues to this day and will, in my opinion, continue for the next fifty years or more. Hispanics in the States report back to their fellow countrymen that, notwithstanding the hardships, life here is better than at home. A wall will not and cannot stop this flow.

Hispanics have become a powerful demographic force. The time has come to recognize that they are here to stay.

And *because* Hispanics are here to stay, it's all the more important that U.S. policy encourage their assimilation, just as previous immigrant populations were encouraged. Unfortunately, this is not now being done. The education gap mentioned above is the result not only of that five-century siesta but also of a half century of misguided policy. As someone who came to the United States more than six decades ago, I have witnessed firsthand the erosion of educational standards and economic opportunities for Hispanics in America.

First among these economic casualties is a situation I call the "Puerto Rican predicament." According to Nicholas Lemann, in the years 1958 and 1959, nearly eleven thousand children were transferred out of Puerto Rican schools, and almost seven thousand were released from New York to go to school in Puerto Rico.[3] Lemann cited this as a new element in New York's ethnic mosaic: a group unlikely to assimilate to the same degree as others do. This is known, in ethnic policy circles, as the *va y ven* syndrome, the "come and go" syndrome. Those who dispute its existence claim that the heavy air traffic back and forth between New York and San Juan is evidence only that Puerto Ricans visit their relatives a lot, not that they relocate constantly. In fact, in a new preface for the 1970 edition of *Beyond the Melting Pot,* Nathan Glazer and Daniel Patrick Moynihan wrote, "Puerto Ricans are economically and occupationally worse off than Negroes, but one does find a substantial move in the second generation that seems to correspond to what we expected for new groups in the city."[4]

But despite Glazer and Moynihan's claims, as Lemann further observed, after the 1960s evidence of Puerto Rican progress out of poverty evaporated. Puerto Rican median family income dropped during the 1970s. Family structure altered substantially: The number of Puerto Ricans living in families headed by a single, unemployed parent had increased nearly 20 percent by 1980. As this happened, all of New York watched the South Bronx slowly falling apart over the course of those two decades. Jill Jonnes, author of *We're Still Here: The Rise, Fall, and Resurrection of the South Bronx,* wrote:

There was arson commissioned by landlords out for their insurance. . . . Arson was set by welfare recipients who

wanted out of their apartments. . . . Many fires were deliberately set by junkies—and by that new breed of professional, the strippers of buildings, who wanted to clear a
building so they could ransack the valuable copper and
brass pipes, fixtures, and hardware. . . . Fires were set by
firebugs who enjoyed a good blaze and by kids out for
kicks. And some were set by those who got their revenge
with fire, jilted lovers returning with a can of gasoline and
a match.[5]

It will be impossible ever to know exactly the extent of the
damage to housing stock in the Bronx these two decades of de-
cay caused. Lemann guesses between fifty thousand and one
hundred thousand housing units during the 1970s alone. This
produced the long stretches of empty, filthy city blocks for
which the South Bronx had become notorious. There were—
and continue to be—a lot of theories circulating about the
cause of this catastrophe, but I still maintain that much of the
blame must lie squarely on the construction of Co-op City, a
middle-income cooperative housing complex of 15,000 apartments built in the 1970s in the North Bronx, which caused a
massive flight from the Grand Concourse in the heart of the
Bronx. Lemann cites as possibilities excessive strictness of rent
control in New York, welfare, unemployment, and drugs. But
he goes on to conclude that picking a single cause is purely ac-

ademic; people had simply given up on any hopes of maintaining a functional society there. "It is rare," he wrote, "for the veneer of civilization to be eroded so rapidly anywhere during peacetime."

Over these same two decades, Puerto Ricans lost the unskilled jobs that had sustained them economically. New York City as a whole lost hundreds of thousands of jobs during the 1970s. The Puerto Ricans suffered enormously from the flight of much of New York's famed garment industry to the South. Lemann quoted Angelo Falcon, then president of the Institute for Puerto Rican Policy: "What I see is a community that came here and put all its eggs in one basket, namely the garment industry and manufacturing." The traditional family structures also began to dissolve. As my own story illustrates, Puerto Ricans have a very strong tradition of extended and diffuse but closely bound family networks. The damage done to these by the economic problems of New York's Puerto Rican community has been one of the most serious and most lasting social ills besetting them, and one that has worsened the plight of Hispanics in America generally.

Yet Hispanic immigrants *can* thrive in the United States, as the recent influx from the Dominican Republic shows. Since the mid-1970s, Dominicans have been streaming into New York City— mainly to Washington Heights, in northern Manhattan, but also to the South Bronx. Dominicans are known for their industriousness, and many of them are illegal aliens ineligible for any kind of social welfare program; they have gone into the undesirable, illegal, or disorganized end of the labor market, working in sweatshops, driving gypsy cabs, and operating unlicensed after-hours nightclubs and other perilous small businesses. Partly because the Dominican migration is predominantly male and the Puerto Rican family in the South Bronx is predominantly female-headed, Dominican–Puerto Rican marriages and liaisons are becoming common. It seems impossible to doubt that the Dominican migration is partly responsible for any resurgence, present or future, in the South Bronx and in New York's Hispanic world.[6]

Unfortunately, as economic opportunities in the garment industry and in manufacturing vanished, the education system also failed the Hispanic community. In the next chapter, I will relate what I have learned about the policies that have failed American children, but Hispanics most of all.

4

The Politics of Education

IN 1947, SIX YEARS after coming to the United States from
Puerto Rico, I enrolled at Haaren High School in Manhattan.
Since I was Hispanic, administrators there automatically steered
me into a vocational course, airplane mechanics, without in-
forming me that students in those classes were not being prepared for college. Only when a college-bound fellow student
told me that I should be switching to "academic" courses did I
discover that a more rigorous but also more enriching path of
study was possible. Opting for this course, I was able to attend
the City College of New York, where I majored in business
administration and accounting, and became a certified public

accountant. Later I studied at Brooklyn Law School and became a lawyer. Were it not for this lucky break, I might never have escaped the usual dead-end path and never advanced to the middle class.

More than half a century later, the education gap remains the most serious problem Hispanics face in America. Clearly, if more than 50 percent of the Hispanic community do not even have high-school diplomas, their opportunities for advancement in America's technologically advanced society are severely limited. Compounding this problem is the fact that education is not a high priority in the Hispanic community: 37 percent of whites between ages eighteen and twenty-four are enrolled full-time or part-time in college, as opposed to 19 percent of Hispanics. When one takes into account the lifetime value of a bachelor's degree—roughly $2.1 million in 2005 dollars—this disadvantage becomes so severe as to verge on the criminal. And when these children turn seventeen, their parents tell them to go out and find work. Of course, worthwhile jobs with decent prospects rarely tumble into the laps of seventeen-year-olds.

Hispanics must learn how to avoid this path and secure a better future for their community. It is up to their own community members to involve themselves in their local school systems and understand how they work. Hispanics must not count on the school system or any arm of government to orient students. That is *their* responsibility, and the first step should be to recognize that, as a group, Hispanics have failed to assume responsibility for their children's welfare. To be blunt, educating Hispanic children is not the duty of the governmental school system. This is *their* duty, as parents, family members, neighbors, and citizens. Whenever a child is left behind, it is not the fault of the teachers, or the principals, or the school chancellor, or the mayor, or the president. It is *their* fault.

Hispanics have no one to blame but themselves for the disastrous high-school dropout rates of the younger members of their community. Considering the large proportion of students who fail to graduate from high school, their resulting inability to ascend into successful standards of living should surprise no one.

It hardly needs mentioning that Hispanic children's future depends upon their educational achievement. Full participation in American society requires a genuine high-school diploma and a real college education. This is essential not just to earn a living but to achieve the inner security that will enable Hispanic children to participate in mainstream America rather than remain trapped within an underachieving minority group.

A feeling of tranquil confidence may be the most significant by-product of a good education. Most people who lack college degrees tend to feel insecure because they sense that they missed out on something important but elusive. The college-educated usually feel self-assured wherever they may be, because they realize that nobody really knows very much; the true value of a college education is gaining the ability to seek answers to questions you need addressed. This feeling of security provides comfort in new situations and among strangers of whatever background.

New York City's public schools have been bogged down for decades in a political tug-of-war for control of the school board among the mayor and other elected officials, the teachers' union, and assorted community organizations. Power occasionally shifts from one group to another, but basic problems remain unaddressed. No side encourages parental involvement, and whichever group gains control, a new bureaucracy emerges to discourage parental participation.

For example, in the 1960s New York's Board of Education consisted of nine members appointed by the mayor. Many blacks and Hispanics were frustrated by the system's poor record in educating their children. So they pushed the state legislature for a school-decentralization plan. The legislature approved three experimental school districts with large minority populations—in East Harlem, the Lower East Side, and Ocean Hill–Brownsville in Brooklyn.

Rhody McCoy, a black teacher who was named administrator of the governing board of the Ocean Hill–Brownsville district, summarily transferred thirteen white teachers, a few assistant principals, and one principal out of the district without their consent. The teachers' union boss, Albert Shanker, called the transfer an illegal violation of civil-service laws. The result was three citywide strikes, which closed 85 percent of local schools for fifty-five days. These labor actions divided the city racially, because many blacks and Latinos supported the Ocean Hill–Brownsville community leaders, while many white parents backed the teachers' union. The strike was one of the most polarizing in local history.

The result was a decentralization law that made no sense. The nine-member central board appointed by the mayor was replaced by a seven-member board, with two mayoral appointees and one named by each of the five borough presidents. This meant that the mayor did not control the school board, nor did anyone else. The central school board appointed the schools chancellor. However, the central school board shared power with thirty-two community school boards that appointed community school superintendents and principals in elementary and junior high schools. This diffusion of authority made it impossible to establish accountability or responsibility. If no one were in charge, no one could be blamed.

Meanwhile, it was 1968, and the school system was in chaos. The overwhelming majority of students were black and Latino, and more than 50 percent of them failed to graduate from high school. Many of those who got diplomas were not performing at high-school level and required remedial courses before they could begin to receive college credit. There was only one high-school diploma that was of any value—a Regents Diploma—and only a small percentage of black and Latino students earned that distinction.

The tragedy was, everyone knew that the system was failing, yet no one in charge voiced any criticism or proposed remedies— not the central school board, not the chancellor, not the community school boards, not the principals, not the teachers, and especially not the teachers' union. Indeed, today, nearly four decades later, the teachers' unions still vigorously oppose charter schools, vouchers, or any alternatives to the government's public-school monopoly.

This is why I have said that the power struggles for control of the public-school system may give the mayor, the teachers' unions, or the community leaders more or less authority, but they engender no change in the system's actual day-to-day operation. From the viewpoint of parents and students, the status quo prevails. That is why the Hispanic community cannot rely on changes at the top of the educational system.

For the first part of my adult life, I believed that achieving political power for the purposes of social change was the answer for moving that Hispanic community ahead in America. By 1993, I had changed my mind. The big problem that remained was education. We were still struggling over a system that made no sense. Michael Tomasky aptly wrote, in a June 1993 article in the *Nation:*

Anyone who has a child in a public school or who pays attention to the schools knows, for example, that the Rainbow Curriculum, the multicultural project . . . is a long way from being the most important reform the schools need now. . . . Working-class parents—of all colors—see "tolerance" as a bit of a luxury when they have to chip in out of their salaries to buy chalk, erasers and mops. . . . And every year spent fretting about rainbows and not about equity in school funding, or whether high school graduates can actually read and write and think, is a year that the people who send their kids to private schools and who shelter their taxes away from the public schools— and we all know who they are—can pass in leisurely laughter at the circus below them.[1]

By 2000, I had been working with Giuliani on elementary and secondary education over the years since that article was published, and with Governor George Pataki for almost ten years on colleges and universities. So I was in a unique position to understand what was going on in education, from kindergarten all the way up to graduate school.

If we fail in education, we fail everywhere. It has to be our most urgent priority. I was, and I remain, as passionate about education as Rudolph Giuliani was and is about crime. Education was and is my crusade.

5

One Country, Two Languages

"BE CAREFUL WHAT you wish for," the old saying goes, "because you just might get it." I should have heeded that proverbial warning when I began to wish for bilingual education as I arrived in New York City from Puerto Rico. I was eleven and a half years old and had a minimal knowledge of English. I lived on East 104th Street and attended school on 103rd Street between Madison and Fifth avenues. I couldn't speak any English, and the teacher spoke no Spanish. Instead of asking and answering questions about American history or setting and solving problems in math, she and I mostly just stared blankly at each other. I saw that the other kids in the classroom could not speak

English and did not understand what was being taught. I thought, even then, that it would be a good thing if classes were conducted in Spanish and in English, so the students would have a better idea of what was going on. Fortunately for me, within a few months I was sent to live with an uncle in Chicago and then with another uncle in California for almost two years. Since I lived in neighborhoods where there were no Latinos—that is, in Anglophone neighborhoods—I became fluent in English more quickly than I would have if I'd stayed in East Harlem.

When I became a lawyer and entered politics in East Harlem in 1960, I discussed the subject of bilingual education with community leaders and found that, to my delight, others were contemplating the same idea.

In 1960, I joined forces with a woman named Ellen Lurie, who was an educational-reform advocate, and a Puerto Rican woman named Evelina Antonetti, a bilingual-education proponent. Together we held the first public hearings on bilingual education in New York City, in 1962. They were hugely successful and were attended by Robert F. Kennedy, who then was the U.S. attorney general. We proposed giving teachers bonuses if they taught bilingual courses. Of course, in those days these and similar proposals were ignored.

Nevertheless, the bilingual-education movement gained support in the city and nationally. In 1968, Congress added a provision to the Elementary and Secondary Education Act (ESEA) that expressed the need for bilingual education. However, it did not detail what a bilingual program should be, nor did it provide adequate funding to launch one. Many of us believed that the best opportunity for defining and approving a true, nationwide bilingual-education program would arise during ESEA's reauthorization in 1974. So I focused my energies on achieving this objective.

Fortunately, I was elected to the House of Representatives in 1970 and became the first Puerto Rican in the nation's history to serve in Congress. I succeeded, thanks to the support of my colleagues, in being appointed to the Education and Labor Committee, which had jurisdiction over all educational matters. As a committee member, I began to advocate bilingual education as a way to improve the educational performance of Hispanic students, who were then arriving in large numbers, particularly in urban public-school systems. They were already performing poorly and dropping out of high school at an alarming rate.

My argument was that educational achievement occurs when the student understands the language and masters the course content for each grade. If the student does not understand English, he or she cannot learn the course content for any grade and instead has to spend time concentrating on learning English. If students focus on learning English, they will most likely fall behind in course content and will be unprepared to absorb the next grade's course content. The result is that by the time they're fluent in English, they'll be far behind other students in mastering the course content and probably will drop out. Bilingual education enables students to absorb lectures and homework in a language they understand (Spanish) while simultaneously learning to speak English. (My own educational experiences in Chicago and Burbank differed because I lived in English-speaking neighborhoods and was exposed to English outside of school, which is not necessarily the case in El Barrio and other urban Hispanic neighborhoods.)

This was the theory of bilingual education, but my colleagues in Congress wanted to see models of successful bilingual-education programs. I referred them to my friends in the Cuban community in Dade County, Florida, with whom I had good relations, since I shared their opposition to Fidel Castro. I knew that the first wave of Cubans whom Castro deported were predominantly from the middle and upper classes. They established bilingual programs that often were taught by exiled professors from the University of Havana. The quality of instructors was so high and the motivation of the parents and students to retain their Spanish was so strong that anyone who visited their classrooms left impressed. Whenever any of my congressional colleagues asked for proof that bilingual education could work, I told them to get the facts that the Cubans themselves provided or to jet down to Dade County to see for themselves. This often proved persuasive.

I also lobbied my colleagues on the Education and Labor Committee, both Democrats and Republicans, to support the new bilingual-education measure, called Title I. For example, the committee's ranking Republican was Minnesota's Albert Quie. He once said that he could not understand why my people (meaning the Puerto Ricans) could not give up speaking Spanish and learn to speak English. I found his surname unusual, so I looked into his background and learned that he was of Norwegian ancestry. I delved into Norwegian history and discovered that Norway had once been conquered and occupied by Germans.

The next day I told Congressman Quie that I was impressed that his ancestors had refused to abandon their native language, even though they were conquered. Thus, I thought, he might understand why Puerto Ricans, whose native language had been Spanish for more than four hundred years, would not surrender their language when they were conquered by the United States in 1898. Congressman Quie was friendlier to bilingual education after that exchange.

In spite of my efforts and those of my allies, I knew that we did not have enough support in the House to pass the bilingual-education title on a yes-or-no vote. I did not want to risk such a vote, because I knew that Senator Edward Kennedy

(D-Massachusetts) and other senators had the votes to pass it in the upper chamber. My staff had discovered an obscure rule that provided that if an amendment passed one house and was considered and not rejected by the other house, then that amendment could be added to the legislation by a House/Senate conference committee.

My staff met with the staff of Congressman Carl Perkins (D-Kentucky), who chaired the Education and Labor Committee and was sympathetic to bilingual education. We prepared a script we would both read on the House floor that would indicate that I had introduced the bilingual-education title and withdrawn it before it could be voted on, with the understanding that if the Senate passed it, the conference committee would consider it. The script precisely complied with House rules.

When the legislation came up for debate on the House floor, I followed the script we had prepared. I introduced the bilingual-education title and immediately withdrew it before a vote could be taken, on the understanding that a conference committee would consider it if the Senate approved it first. The Senate, under Teddy Kennedy's influence, approved the bilingual-education title, and then a House/Senate conference committee adopted it. Thus, the bilingual-education act became law without ever having been voted upon as a separate title by the House of Representatives, because once it was incorporated into the total ESEA of 1974, individual yes/no votes on the bill's separate sections were forbidden.

The 1974 amendment to the Bilingual Education Act provides that there shall be instruction in English and, to the extent necessary to enable the student to participate effectively in a course of study, the pupil's native language. Therefore, the basic requirements are these:

1. Instruction in English and in Spanish (or whatever other language may be involved). That's what *bi*lingualism means—*two* languages.
2. A limited period—not specified but understood, since the purpose is to enable students to participate along with regular students; once they do, the instruction continues in English.

This is where the saying "Be careful what you wish for, because you just might get it" comes in. We all thought in 1974 that it was clear that the purpose of bilingual education was to enable students to learn to speak English without missing out on course content. It was obvious to me and to all of us that the program would continue for a limited time only—we did not specify for *how* long, because we believed educators should decide that.

The reality of what has occurred since 1974 has been a complete distortion of the bilingual-education law. New York City began at that time to develop an array of programs to teach children everything from math to history in their native languages. Federal education aid provided incentives for schools to expand these programs by giving them aid for each student referred to bilingual education. Since the mid-1980s, enrollment in programs for city students labeled "limited English proficient," and thereby eligible for federal aid, nearly doubled, from 85,000 students to 154,000. Bilingual programs are available not only in Spanish but in Chinese, Haitian Creole, Russian, Korean, Vietnamese, French, Greek, Arabic, and Bengali.

Bilingual programs had come under mounting criticism from educators, state officials, and civil-rights groups, like the Mexican American Legal Defense and Educational Fund, for failing generations of children whose first language was not English. In New York City, many parents and educators had criticized the manner in which students are channeled into bilingual programs. From kindergarten on, every student whose parent has a Hispanic last name or who specifies on a questionnaire that a foreign language is sometimes spoken at home was required to take an English-language test each year. Students who scored below the fortieth percentile were automatically assigned to bilingual classes if the school had at least fifteen students of that language group and grade. Students assigned to an English-as-a-second-language program (ESL) received training aimed only at teaching them English. Bilingual students received some training in English but got a significant part of their instruction, if not most of it, in their native language.

Reexamining bilingual education, the Board of Education released a study concluding that efforts to educate tens of thousands of students in their native languages were flawed. The study found that students—even recent immigrants—who took most of their classes in English generally fared better academically than did students in bilingual programs, where little English is spoken.

Luis O. Reyes, the board's Manhattan representative, noted that the goals of the board's special language programs included "native language development" as well as learning English quickly. Thus, in many jurisdictions in New York City and throughout the country, *bi*lingual education became, as I said, *mono*lingual education—not in English but in Spanish, or whatever the other language might be. Furthermore, even where instruction was bilingual, schools have been found in which bilingual education has continued for eight years!

The worst single example of this type of abuse came to my attention some years ago when I was Mayor Giuliani's special counsel. One of my friends on the Board of Education called to tell me that he had received a directive from the schools chancellor to register thirty bilingual teachers who had just arrived from Spain. The thirty teachers came down to his personnel office to be registered as bilingual teachers *with a translator*—because they could not speak English! They were duly registered, because these were the instructions from the chancellor's office. Upon inquiry I discovered that the chancellor's office had advertised for bilingual teachers in Latin American countries. What usually happened under this arrangement is that once the "bilingual" teachers learned to speak English, they went back to their native country to teach English.

Efforts to eliminate bilingual education have failed, even though it is clear that as it is being taught at present, bilingual education does not work and may in fact prevent Hispanic kids from performing well in school. The most famous reform attempt was Proposition 277, which was adopted in California in 1998. Proposition 277 required that all instruction in the public schools be in English, with exceptions only in the most extreme cases, and permitted parents to sue to ensure that the rule was enforced. Its main supporter was software entrepreneur Ron Unz. He was inspired by an Episcopal priest and community activist named Alice Callaghan, who staged a walkout at the Ninth Street Elementary School in Los Angeles because its students had little access to English instruction.

Prop 277 was originally adopted to remedy the problem that California public schools have in educating immigrant children, traditionally wasting their financial resources on costly experimental language programs that have, over the past two decades, failed to combat immigrant children's high dropout rates and low English-literacy levels. Although test scores have steadily improved since its implementation, Prop 277 has shown limited results. While bilingual education continues in California, there remains a powerful body of research that proves that immersion techniques do in fact work. Bilingual education requires an average of four to seven years before students master English, but immersion programs accelerate that to as little as one year. Immersion's benefits are most dramatic for immigrant children in the early grades.

Also, there is the problem of measuring results. Studies that compare immersion techniques to bilingual education have had trouble controlling for outside influences. Thus, while Prop 277 may not appear to be doing much, there are no definitive data that say bilingual education could achieve more. In fact, in the decades when bilingual education was the norm, fewer than 40 percent of non-English-speaking students actually achieved fluency after ten years in California schools.

The bilingual program is not nearly as rigid as initially feared. Parents who want their children to receive bilingual education may obtain opt-in waivers. Largely, however, this option has not been taken advantage of. This is in part because anecdotal evidence shows that the end of bilingual education, at the very least, does not negatively affect the ability of students to learn. There also appear to be only very limited effects on class participation. And despite rules on the amount of Spanish that can be spoken in the classroom (no more than 20 percent), teachers have found new and innovative ways of incorporating the Latino culture into their lessons.

Supporters of Prop 277 claim that the deficiencies are not a result of the program itself but of improper implementation. It is suggested that teachers receive increased training in how to educate non–English speakers and that they place emphasis on activities that rely heavily on language, such as writing and discussion, rather than on having students listen to lectures.

Ron Unz has attempted to have the equivalent of Prop 277 adopted in New York and other states, but without success. Bilingual education is alive and well in California, though.

There are also some legal and practical reasons that it may be impossible to eliminate bilingual education. The most important legal reason is the case of *Lau v. Nichols* (414 U.S. 563), decided by the U.S. Supreme Court in 1974. This was a class-action suit brought by non-English-speaking Chinese students against officials in a San Francisco school district, seeking relief against unequal educational opportunities. The state of California's Education Code provided that no pupil shall receive a diploma of graduation from grade twelve who has not met the standards of proficiency in English as well as other prescribed subjects. The Court, in an opinion written by Justice William O. Douglas, held that under these state-imposed standards there is no equality of treatment merely by providing students with the same facilities, textbooks, teachers and curriculum; for students who do not understand English are effectively foreclosed from any meaningful education.

Basic English skills are at the very core of what these public schools teach. Imposition of a requirement that, before a child can effectively participate in the educational program, he must already have acquired those basic skills is to make a mockery of public education. We know that those who do not understand English are certain to find their classroom experiences wholly incomprehensible and in no way meaningful.

It seems obvious that the Chinese-speaking minority receive fewer benefits than the English-speaking majority from respondents' school system which denies them a meaningful opportunity to participate in the educational program—all earmarks for the discrimination banned by the regulations.

It would appear from this decision that imposition of an immersion system that teaches only English would foreclose the students "from any meaningful education" and that "those who do not understand English are certain to find their classroom experiences wholly incomprehensible and in no way meaningful."

In any event, any attempt to eliminate bilingual education would face a difficult course in view of the *Lau* decision.

Another legal obstacle is the consent decree in the federal case of *Aspira of New York, Inc. v. the Board of Education of the City of New York.* It requires "instruction in substantive courses in Spanish (i.e., courses in mathematics, science and social studies) which is to say, a child is not to receive instruction in any substantive courses in a language which prevents his/her effective participation in any such course rather than in a language in which he/she can more effectively participate." This consent decree cannot be modified unless Aspira agrees, and that is most unlikely.

The practical reasons bilingualism is unlikely to be reversed are political. There is a huge lobby of bilingual educators, backed by the teachers' unions, who would fight such a move and would get strong political support from Hispanic parents who have been persuaded that bilingual education is important in order to preserve Hispanic culture.

The most practical solution to the problem of bilingualism is the "dual language" approach, which seems to be gaining adherents. This program integrates students who are native English speakers in classes with native speakers of another language and provides instruction to both groups in both languages. Unlike the transitional bilingual program, where the goal is to make a quick shift to English using the native language, the goal of the dual-language program is for all students to become proficient in two languages. Of course, this is a lengthy process, but at least it has as its goal that students learn to speak and write English, at least some of the time.

Absent such programs, however, the outcome that many of us wished for when we fought for bilingualism—increasing both the educational opportunities for Hispanics and their assimilation into mainstream America—will remain an elusive dream.

But bilingualism is only one of the harmful practices in America's school systems that create almost insurmountable obstacles to Hispanic progress. Unlike bilingualism, however, these other practices, including "social promotion," are not widely publicized, and many parents do not even know that they exist. In the next chapter, therefore, I will describe in detail these other practices, against which parents and policy makers must be eternally vigilant.

6

Social Promotion and Other Implements of Ignorance

NEW YORK CITY and many urban centers with large proportions of Hispanic and other minority students practice "social
promotion." This means that students are promoted automatically from one grade to the next, whether they learn anything or
not. If you do your work, you pass. If you don't do your work,
you pass. Nobody fails. Children are promoted not for educational reasons but for social reasons—that is, because they grow
one year older, not necessarily wiser.

The concept of social promotion in the public schools sprang
from purely political motives—namely, the fear of the system's
being called racist if black and Latino students receive failing
grades and are required to repeat their courses.

There was a time when New York City's population was overwhelmingly white. Students and teachers alike were largely white, and standards and discipline were enforced in the school system. In those days parents accepted the judgment of teachers and principals, and students who did not perform in school were left back. Sometime in the 1940s and 1950s, the city's school population began to change. Large numbers of black and Latino students whose parents had moved to New York from the American South or from Puerto Rico entered the school system. Unlike the advent of open admissions at CUNY—which can be traced to a violent student strike at City College in April 1969— the exact date when social promotion went into effect cannot be traced to a particular incident.

Even as more and more students happened to be black or Latino, teachers remained overwhelmingly white. There were not nearly enough blacks or Latinos enrolled in colleges, fewer still who received degrees in education and passed the teachers' exam. White teachers were afraid of being branded as racists if they failed black and Latino students.

Thus the decision was made, without any public discussion, to advance pupils from one grade to the next regardless of performance. The term "social promotion" was devised to conceal what was really political cowardice. Worst of all, politicians accepted the charade and never confronted what in essence was a dismantling of the educational system.

The intellectual justification for social promotion was that it was sociologically harmful for children to be left back and that their self-esteem would be injured if such a thing happened. I have never found any sociologist who defended this outrageous nonsense. I have always said that sociologically, the only thing worse for a child than repeating failed grades is to be seventeen years old and unable to read, write, or compute.

Moreover, since social promotion is applied primarily to black and Latino children, the underlying premise is that these children cannot learn as well as white children can and therefore some shortcut must be used to ease them through the school system. This is the most scandalous—albeit unspoken—justification for social promotion, because the consequences of allowing students to pass from one grade to the next without any real learning is that they are doomed to remain incapable of performing any meaningful job or participating in any significant way in this advanced society.

The education establishment still pushes the idea of social promotion as beneficial to minorities. The opposite, in fact, is the case. Social promotion is, to be blunt, one of the most covertly racist philosophies ever conceived of in education policy, a field with a long history of serious mistakes.

Social promotion is bogus, patronizing compassion. It's rooted in a fear that black and Hispanic students cannot meet rigorous educational standards. What should be the fundamental, immovable assumption of any educational enterprise is that people will rise, or sink, to the level of expectations they encounter—just as I did. It's true that because of the great variation in ability and talent from individual to individual, not everyone will achieve at the same level. However, if you want to be an accountant, two plus two equals four, no matter what color you are.

Look at artists and entertainers. These are unquestionably professions in which personal merit and talent count above all else: if you can't sing, you can't sing. No one advocates affirmative action for singers, actors, musicians, or dancers. No one advocates it for baseball players either: They can bat, run, and field or they can't. Blacks, who have enjoyed fantastic success in these areas, have shown that they clearly can perform at the level of any other ethnic group. So why should they, or any other disadvantaged group, be held to lower standards in school, where talent is less important than hard work and diligence? Talent may be innate, but anyone with enough determination can become a success academically.

Sadly, in large part the persistence of social promotion, in the face of its absurdity, stems from liberal white guilt and fear. Teachers are afraid to flunk black and Hispanic kids because of the demonizing accusations of racism that will surely follow.

The education establishment is caught up in racial politics. Things have reached such a desperate pass that almost any kind of serious educational norm is labeled "elitist."[1] Thirty years ago, when New York's school population changed to become overwhelmingly black and Hispanic, nearly all of the teachers were white. They couldn't take the racial heat. They didn't want to face being accused of racism by black and Hispanic parents. To explain away the phenomenon of passing underperforming students, the education establishment came up with the theory of social promotion, claiming that it is sociologically bad for children to repeat grades. I asked, repeatedly, who the sociologists were that had reached this conclusion, and I was never given a substantive answer. As with so much in the history of education theory in New York, the establishment backed down at the slightest hint of controversy.

The truth is, if a student receives a high-school diploma on the principle that "if you're breathing, you'll pass," that diploma is worthless. As one black student in New York City put it, "I got a diploma doing nothing." This problem will continue as long as the high schools practice social promotion.

The truth is, if anything, it's "racist" *not* to hold minority students to the same standards as others.[2] Inadequate preparation also results from lower expectations and from the notion that lowering the bar will somehow help minority students. This is a prescription for failure, pure and simple.

I never accepted social promotion, and I was the leading advocate for its elimination. And while the politically correct thing to say is that the bar should be lowered for blacks and Latinos, I resent that, as a proud Hispanic. As I said, I competed with other students and still came out on top.

The first time I tried to abolish social promotion was in 1978, when I became deputy mayor in the Koch administration. Technically I was "Deputy Mayor of Management," but I had narrowed my responsibilities to two issues: rebuilding the South Bronx and restructuring the school system. These were gigantic tasks in themselves, but I felt prepared for these challenges. I had been a housing commissioner and therefore understood urban renewal. I had served in Congress on the House Education and Labor Committee and had spent years examining educational programs in urban centers and nationwide.

In March 1978, Schools Chancellor Irving Anker called to tell me he was resigning and, as a present to me, had issued an order abolishing social promotion. I was delighted and immediately developed a program called Educational Gates. I proposed that students who did their work and met grade-level standards would get promoted; those who did not would stay back but receive focused help in special classes. That is to say, they would not be left behind to repeat a grade with younger kids. Instead they would receive remedial assistance in their own special classes. Once they made up their work, they would be promoted. Those were the gates, and they applied to every grade from one to twelve.

I had wanted Congresswoman Shirley Chisholm to be the new schools chancellor. For one thing, we agreed on the need to eliminate social promotion. Also, she was an African-American woman who would relate extraordinarily well with black students and parents. Alas, Mayor Koch believed she was too strong a personality and probably thought he had a strong enough personality in me without adding another one to the mix. So he chose Frank Macchiarola, who in fact became an excellent chancellor.

The responsibility for defending Educational Gates fell on my shoulders, however. I was the one who had argued so passionately that social promotion was hurting black and Hispanic students and that we had to eliminate it. When we brought in the new schools chancellor, Frank Macchiarola, he agreed with me.

Under Koch, as I said, I was in charge of selling this program to the community of black and Hispanic parents. Friends and colleagues warned me that while I could say publicly to Hispanics that their children were underperforming because I was Puerto Rican, I wouldn't dare say it to black parents.

The syndrome wasn't new, and I wasn't the first victim. People whose proposals—particularly in the area of education—directly challenge the failed policies of the past were inevitably belittled as "betrayers" of their community's interests. Justice Clarence Thomas was branded a "race traitor" for his conservative opinions. Gary Franks, as the only black Republican in

Congress, was actually barred from membership in the Congressional Black Caucus because he didn't march in ideological lockstep with its members.

Ward Connerly, the black University of California regent who spearheaded a national campaign for race-neutral college admissions, received similar treatment. In a *60 Minutes* interview, Mike Wallace charged that Connerly was perceived as a "traitor" by "many people in the black community" and even trotted out Connerly's cousin to denounce his "minstrel show."[3]

But I responded to my critics: "Watch me." I went into a community meeting in Brooklyn and told the black parents that their children would fail and be held back if they didn't live up to the educational standards set by the Gates program. And—surprise, surprise—the parents agreed with me. The result was that Chancellor Macchiarola successfully implemented Educational Gates, and there was no political backlash whatsoever.

After I left City Hall, Chancellor Macchiarola, caving to public pressure from the teachers' union, restricted the Gates program to grades four and seven only. This was a mistake. If you wait until the fourth grade to enforce standards, it's too late for many students. They will never catch up. But at least the Educational Gates concept remained in place. Unfortunately, when Chancellor Macchiarola resigned, the Gates program began to erode. When David Dinkins became mayor in 1989, the program was eliminated completely, and New York quietly reimposed social promotion.

When Rudolph W. Giuliani became mayor in 1994 and I served as his special counsel on education, he gave an educational speech that outlined these five goals:

- higher standards
- the elimination of social promotion
- better security, including assigning school safety to the NYPD
- reduced bureaucracy
- reorganization of the school system

What Mayor Giuliani wanted was control of the school system, which, of course, he did not get, since it had been denied to Mayors Koch and Dinkins. State legislators from New York City wanted to preserve a system shot through with patronage, corruption, and cronyism. Gotham's public-school system was the nation's largest. Its budget in 1994 was almost $8 billion: It included 1,016,728 students, 66,989 teachers, and 86,989 other employees.

The central school board had seven members—two appointed by the mayor and five appointed by individual borough presidents. The mayor controlled neither the school board nor the schools.

Moreover, the central board shared powers with community

school boards that appointed community superintendents and school principals. An example of corruption at that level arose when I received a tape recording of a South Bronx school board meeting convened to select certain principals. Four board members said they would vote only for principals who were black or Latino. Four others said they would vote for any person for principal, provided they (the board members) received some benefit in return. A ninth member said she was running for City Council and would vote only for a prospective principal who would contribute to her campaign. I forwarded the tape to the special investigator for schools. Years later he indicted a school-board member who was recorded accepting a payoff for an appointment. Unfortunately, it took plenty of work to arrange one indictment. I am certain that many such illegal acts escaped prosecution, as did the other crimes I heard on that recording.

In April 1994, Mayor Giuliani became dissatisfied with Schools Chancellor Ramon Cortines, a Dinkins holdover, because Cortines could not give satisfactory answers about the $8 billion school-board budget. Cortines famously could not answer this question of Giuliani's: How many employees work at 110 Livingston Street, the old school-board headquarters in Brooklyn? Cortines had no idea how many people worked for him under his own roof! Giuliani summoned Chancellor Cortines to Gracie Mansion and gave him twenty-four hours to appoint a deputy chancellor for fiscal management, or else

Giuliani would appoint me as his special counsel for the fiscal oversight of education. As a CPA, the mayor explained, I understood finances.

Those twenty-four hours passed, and Cortines took no action. Giuliani announced that I would be the school system's new fiscal monitor. Cortines announced his resignation effective July 1. This threw the city into turmoil. However, Governor Mario Cuomo intervened to mediate the dispute, and Cortines rescinded his resignation. He agreed to my appointment as special counsel, which was an unpaid position. Subsequently I met with Chancellor Cortines, who explained to me that he would cooperate with me but that the board's five computer systems had to be consolidated before he could provide me with information. I asked how long it would take to compile the necessary information.

"Three years," he replied.

I said, "We don't have three years. We need an answer now."

I reported our conversation to Giuliani and offered to get some of my friends from Coopers & Lybrand, a well-known national accounting firm, to produce the information. They deployed a virtual platoon of auditors to examine the board's vast financial system and discovered that the board used at least 277,000 different ledger accounts to track spending in its thirty-five divisions, bureaus, and offices and thirty-two local school districts.

They discovered also that the board spent $18,705 on each special-education student in 1993. By 1994, special ed consumed nearly 25 cents out of every education dollar we spent. Because of the high levels of expenditure on special education, the city was spending only between $3,500 and $5,000 on each student in regular classrooms, far less than the $7,900 that school officials usually cited as an average. Special ed, in other words, was draining money from students in regular classrooms. Actually, per-pupil spending in New York City for regular students was more like the level in Alabama, where about $3,600 was spent, than that in suburban districts like Nassau and Westchester counties, where the rate was about $12,000 per student.

The study—prepared by Coopers & Lybrand, using the 277,000 separate budget items supplied by the Board of Education for the fiscal year that ended in June—broke down spending into categories for such things as instruction, instructional structure, operations, and centralized administration. The study showed that the city directed a smaller portion of school dollars into the classroom compared to such other costs as busing, lunches, security, and debt, which chewed up larger portions of the budget.

We found that the actual spending on books, pencils, paper, and other classroom supplies came to only $44 per student. By contrast, the system spent $788 per pupil on its administration at the central and district levels. Not enough of the board's budget made it to the classroom. Nationally, other schools averaged

62.5 percent of their budgets on instruction, considerably more than the 47.8 percent in New York. Educators said that this gap was attributable to the unique needs of the New York City system—for handicapped children, school security, transportation, bilingual instruction, breakfasts and lunches for impoverished children—and the complex administrative organization, with a central headquarters, a high-school division, and thirty-two local school districts.[4] While the city schools spent $7,918 for each of 1,016,728 schoolchildren, the average dropped to $4,287 for the majority of students not enrolled in special education or bilingual programs. Of that amount, only $2,308 was spent on teaching.

The school system had become so hydra-headed, so top-heavy with administrators, that even statistics offered by the board itself were not clear as to how many people are included in the annual budget, or even where the money went. By all estimates, however, a disproportionate amount was spent on the bureaucracy instead of in the classroom. According to the board's own figures, there were an average of 5.8 educational administrators for every 1,000 students, compared with 3.4 in the rest of the state, and 23.5 nonteachers for every 100 teachers in the public-school system, compared with 17.8 in the rest of the state.

"The smart folk will tell you it's like Vietnam," said John Elwell, director of the Center for Educational Innovation at the Manhattan Institute, of the budgetary state of the schools. "You go in and you can't get out. You can't make it work."[5] We really had to reform the system. We couldn't do it by magic. There needed to be an independent fiscal monitor to make sure the money that needed to be spent on kids in the classroom actually *was* spent on kids.

Cortines announced he was resigning and would leave office by October 15, if not sooner. He notified the president of the Board of Education in a two-sentence note after Rudy announced the formation of a commission to investigate the school system's handling of safety and violence. Cortines said he had made up his mind in part because he felt he was hurting the system by staying on. Dinkins, union leaders, and bureaucrats described Cortines's departure as a "disaster."[6] The *Village Voice* speculated, "The chancellor may well have understood that it was either resign or risk surprise handcuffs."

After this unpleasant publicity, James Barron wrote in the *New York Times* that "Cortines is haunted . . . by a ghost chancellor . . . : Herman Badillo." I was "not the chancellor yet," Cortines had petulantly informed the Board of Education. But he was growing "a little tired" of me. "Everything that comes up, he tends to be all-knowing," Cortines said of me. But I did not want to be chancellor, and I had never attacked Cortines personally. I was just trying to get the facts, to report them to the mayor and the public.

Cortines was replaced by Rudolph Crew, an experienced

black educator from Washington State. The first time I met Chancellor Crew, I told him we had to eliminate social promotion and establish standards. I said that since he was black and I was Puerto Rican, the most important contribution we could make to our respective communities was to ensure that young people would be prepared to achieve as adults. He told me he agreed but that it would take time to remove social promotion.

The years went by, and Dr. Crew took no action to eliminate social promotion. In the meantime, as we suggested, he accepted the presence of NYPD officers in the schools. This had become an issue because crime was rising on many campuses. I once told Mayor Giuliani that I had visited a Bronx high school whose principal opened up his desk drawer to show me its contents. It was packed with guns and knives. He informed me that he had confiscated these weapons from his students. I told him that when I went to law school, I learned that possessing an unlicensed gun was a felony and that there was no such thing as confiscation without punishment. The principal just shrugged his shoulders. Principals obviously did not report all the crimes that occurred at their schools because they didn't want those episodes reflected on their own personnel records.

Giuliani insisted that school security guards who reported to principals could not be trusted to take appropriate police action when crimes were committed. Despite strong political opposition, Giuliani finally succeeded in getting city policemen assigned to the schools. The public could rest assured that students would enjoy true school safety.

Giuliani kept pressing the state legislature to abolish the cumbersome central school board and the multifarious community boards and grant him complete control of the school system—all without success.

Suddenly, in late 1999, Chancellor Crew announced that he was going to eliminate social promotion. I knew then that Crew would resign by year's end, since I doubted he had the stomach to join the fight for standards. Sure enough, Crew was gone by the end of the year. A new chancellor, Harold O. Levy, a white banking executive with ties to the Democratic Party, moved into the job. He took no strong action to enforce standards and essentially served as caretaker chancellor until the 2001 mayoral election.

In June 2001, I announced that I was running for mayor of New York City as a Republican. One of the strongest planks in my platform was the permanent abolition of social promotion, the establishment of standards, and the restructuring of the school system.

Unfortunately for me, Michael Bloomberg—a businessman who had built a multinational financial media company and who was worth $5 billion personally—also announced he was running for mayor on the Republican line. He admitted that he had been an active, generous Democrat and was running as a Republican only because he did not think he could win as a

Democrat. Bloomberg received Governor Pataki's support and that of all the biggest GOP contributors. Mayor Giuliani remained publicly neutral, although his supporters campaigned for Bloomberg. I lost the Republican primary, since Bloomberg spent tons of his own money and I, as a confirmed nonbillionaire, could not match his resources. Michael Bloomberg went on to spend over $70 million and defeat Democrat Mark Green for mayor in November 2001.

Mayor Bloomberg was not as polarizing a figure as Mayor Giuliani had been, and he quietly succeeded in persuading the state legislature to give him control of the public-school system in June 2002. He abolished the central school board, dumped the community school boards, and completely reorganized the school bureaucracy. He established a Department of Education and appointed Joel Klein commissioner of education, a position that reported directly to the mayor. Klein had served in Bill Clinton's Justice Department as antitrust chief and later became CEO of Bertelsmann, the German media giant. The mayor announced that he was going to improve student performance and that he expected to be judged by his ability to do so when he ran for reelection in 2005. Observers widely and properly regarded this as a courageous move.

During the 2001 Republican primary, Bloomberg and I debated on television and agreed that, if elected, we would abolish social promotion. After Mayor Bloomberg took control of the school system in 2002 and once the schools were reorganized, I reminded the mayor of our agreement to end social promotion. In spring 2003, the mayor invited me to his State of the City speech in Queens. He announced that he was eliminating social promotion in the third grade, and that he was doing so after discussions with me. In 2004, he announced that he would eliminate social promotion in the fifth grade, and in 2005 he announced that he was eliminating social promotion in the seventh grade.

When students were tested in 2005, the year Mayor Bloomberg ran for reelection, the results showed significant improvement in grade-level achievement. Published polls showed that Bloomberg's most popular initiative was the elimination of social promotion. I became cochairman of Mayor Bloomberg's reelection campaign, shot commercials on his behalf in English and Spanish, and campaigned vigorously for his reelection because all his opponents attacked him as being too tough on students. Apparently they still do not support standards. As the *New York Post* editorialized on September 5, 2005:

Social promotion is a disservice to children—sending them on to the next grade utterly unprepared for the work that will be asked of them. Research shows that most of these kids *never* catch up.

And letting kids who can't even meet the already low standards move up a grade based on teacher evaluations—well, that's just criminal.

Yet, nevertheless, most Dems are grousing that Bloomberg is too tough.

What opponents don't seem to understand is that making sure kids can meet standards isn't mean or "punishing" or coldhearted.

It is a fundamental prerequisite for learning. And anyone who's unwilling to enforce these necessary standards is unfit to be mayor.

I would have preferred, of course, that social promotion be eliminated in every grade immediately and that the other educational reforms I had discussed with the mayor and chancellor be adopted. I would also have greatly preferred to see social promotion eliminated long before the fourth grade, when the damage has already been done. But I was nonetheless pleased that dramatic, permanent steps to improve the school system had finally been taken. I believe that even more dramatic action to inspire student achievement will not emerge until parents demand it.

Tracking

Most Hispanic parents do not know that in New York City and in many urban school systems schools are segregated by ability. In practice this fosters racial segregation. In New York City, there is a category of classes known as "special programs," or SP. The children in these classes perform at or above grade level. They are predominantly white, non-Hispanic children and Asians in schools with large Asian populations.

There is another category of instruction within the same schools that is called "academic classes." These courses, their misleading name notwithstanding, are for students who perform poorly in school. These boys and girls are predominantly Hispanic and black. The instruction level and the entire curriculum in these classes are inferior to those in the SP classes. Therefore a student who does well in academic classes gets an inferior education and will continue to endure subpar instruction throughout his or her school years.

In an unusually candid article, the April 3, 2005, *New York Times* discussed a tracking school in Maplewood, New Jersey, that the paper described as segregated. Here is how the article opened:

Columbia High School seems to have it all—great sports teams, great academics, famous alumni and an impressive campus with Gothic buildings. But no one boasted about one aspect of this blue-ribbon school, that its classrooms are largely segregated.

Though the school is majority black, white students make up the bulk of the advanced classes, while black students far outnumbered whites in lower-level classes, statistics show.

"It's kind of sad," said Ugoshi Opara, a senior who is president of the student council. "You can tell right away, just by looking into a classroom, what level it is."

This is the reality of many high schools coast to coast and one of the side effects of aggressive leveling, the increasingly popular practice of dividing students into ability groups.

The practice of tracking students within a school is not limited to high schools but extends to elementary and middle schools as well, although the media usually overlook this. Parents have to be alert, because these schools never are identified as segregated. They may be divided between academic and vocational courses.

At Haaren High School, my alma mater, no one informed any of us that the vocational classes, where blacks and Puerto Ricans were placed, were dead-end courses, whereas the then correctly labeled academic classrooms led to college, knowledge, and prosperity. Whatever principals or teachers tell parents about why their children are assigned to particular classes, parents can always figure out what is really afoot simply by looking at all the classrooms at their kids' schools. If the classes are divided predominantly by race, the school is segregated, no matter what fancy words school administrators assign to various levels of academic performance.

Moreover, students understand there are lower expectations in some courses than in others within the same grade. I know of one middle-school language-arts instructor who teaches both lower-level and advanced courses. However, she teaches the same demanding curriculum to both groups.

On the first day of class, she tells the lower-level students that she will teach them the same material she offers her high-level classes. The "inferior" students invariably ask, "You mean we're going to do the same work as the smart students?"

"Yes, you will," the teacher replies.

The advanced curriculum includes such classics as John Steinbeck's *Of Mice and Men,* Harper Lee's *To Kill a Mockingbird,* and William Shakespeare's *Romeo and Juliet* and *A Midsummer Night's Dream.* Invariably the black and Hispanic students rise to meet these higher expectations. In a recent Shakespeare festival that this teacher staged in the school auditorium, a black student portrayed Romeo while a Hispanic student presented a video he recorded in Central Park in which his fellow students performed *A Midsummer Night's Dream.* Students produced and directed these efforts with no help from their teacher. Remember: These are the kids who supposedly were incapable of performing at more advanced levels!

Parents must not accept segregated schools under any

circumstances. Such arrangements guarantee that their children will endure inferior instruction. Parents must demand that top school-district administrators encourage racial integration while improving school quality. This is not impossible, as one district in Brooklyn has done both. This means installing effective principals who attract more able teachers. But it also means that parents must bring their concerns to the media. Otherwise the status quo will continue to weld young minds shut.

Parents must examine the social makeup of each classroom in the school and inspect the books that are given to the students in each class. If pupils are not performing well enough to enter classes that provide real education, parents must provide special tutoring to enable their children to move into the classrooms where real education does take place.

Vocational Schools

Another species of tracking is particularly misleading because it sounds so appealing: vocational schools. This label impresses Hispanic parents and students because it suggests that jobs await students immediately upon high-school graduation. The problem is that there is no guarantee that any jobs actually exist or that the high school will make any effort to provide them. I once visited a South Bronx vocational high school that specialized in construction trades. Over two thousand students, all blacks and Latinos, trained to become carpenters, plumbers, bricklayers, and electricians. I asked the principal if he was aware that the construction unions discriminated against blacks and Latinos and that very few of the two thousand kids, if they graduated, would be able to find work. The principal said that he was aware of the problem but that it was a political issue, one that would be settled by elected officials, not educators. This principal even went so far as to say outright that this disconnect was not his problem. It was, however, my problem. "You're the politician," I remember him insisting. "If the unions won't take them, that's not my problem. I'm the principal; teachers teach them what to do, and we turn them out. Whether they get a job or not, that's not for us to worry about." In later years I would come to consider this the height of educational irresponsibility.

The worst single example of vocational education I can cite was my own experience as a student at Haaren High School. Haaren offered vocational courses to students in West Harlem, where I then lived. As I mentioned earlier, I found myself there studying airplane mechanics. I learned how to dismantle internal combustion engines, build model airplanes, and draw aircraft blueprints. I gleaned plenty of the complexities of propeller-driven airplanes. I found it all interesting but not particularly challenging.

The sad and, to me, unforgivable part of this story is that no teacher or counselor in the Board of Education ever advised or even suggested to me that I matriculate in college. If I had not joined the school newspaper, where a fellow student virtually invited me onto the academic track, I probably would have wound up with a degree in airplane mechanics. This would have been worthless even in 1947, as jet engines quickly were replacing the internal combustion engines we were studying.

It infuriates me to this day that blacks and Puerto Ricans automatically are assigned to nonacademic courses. Moreover, I am not convinced that this practice has stopped even now. There may be fewer technical courses, but I don't believe that the average black or Puerto Rican middle-school student receives any kind of academic orientation at all. My suspicion is reinforced by the fact that 50 percent of black and Latino students today do not even receive high-school diplomas.

The most enraging aspect of my experience at Haaren High School is that the same internal combustion airplane engines are *still* used today at the High School for Marine and Aviation Trades in Queens. I've spent *over forty years* trying to retire these antiques from the New York City school system, to no avail.

When I became Bronx borough president in 1966, I had the right to appoint a member to the central Board of Education. In the late 1960s, I told my appointee that the only thing I wanted from him was to remove those airplane engines from Haaren High, since nobody used internal combustion engines anymore;

the boys who learned to maintain them would be unemployable. Each year I asked him if those engines were gone, and each year he said no.

Nearly twenty years later, at the Westchester County Airport, I was returning from a trip with a wealthy law client from Texas who had some business interests there. He asked me if I knew anyone at the New York City Board of Education. I told him that my friend was the chancellor of the school system. My client told me that he was the national chairman of the Antique Airplanes Association and that every so often its members flew planes with antique internal combustion engines. He had heard there were some beautiful ones at the Aviation High School in Queens. His organization was willing to exchange them for modern jet engines and make a financial contribution to the Board of Education.

I called the schools chancellor, who joined my client and me at the Aviation High School. We met the principal. He showed us the same airplane engines on which I had worked as a student forty years earlier. There they were, still ruining young people's lives. Moreover, the principal explained, there were no jet engines on the premises to teach students marketable skills. This was in the 1980s, when a 747 was about as exotic as a school bus. We had several subsequent meetings, but nothing happened.

Finally the chancellor called to inform me that nothing could be done. The decision was that in order to instruct students on jet engines, *teachers* would have to be trained for three years on jet engines, and the city could not afford to do so.

So the obsolete old engines are still there, a symbol of bureaucratic obstinacy. It's no wonder that so many people, including alumni like me, have nothing but contempt for the bureaucracy of the New York City school system. In the course of my political career, I found many other instances of young people being trained for nonexistent jobs and being given no guidance to help them achieve meaningful careers. Truly, in New York City today, if you are black or Latino, the search for a worthwhile education is a monumental struggle.

Schools for Gifted Children

Another technique frequently used is a separate curriculum for "gifted children." The philosophy behind this is that there is a special group of children who are superior intellectually to normal children and that they merit unique instruction. The problem with this theory is that when the curriculum is analyzed, it turns out not to be special at all. The noted educational historian Diane Ravitch has explained this as follows:

What we now call "gifted" describes the kind of curriculum that the schools used to offer all students. The Junior

Great Books program, for example, usually offered only to gifted classes, looks very much like that regular curriculum of the 1930s and 1940s. Parents are just frightened to see their children consigned to the dumbed-down miscellany that has become the norm.

White, middle-class parents immediately understand what Ravitch means when she speaks of the norm as a dumbed-down curriculum. They insist that all their children be placed in classes for "gifted" children. Otherwise they threaten to leave the public-school system. Hispanic parents believe that there are massive numbers of gifted children and do not object when the middle-class kids are put in these special classes. They do not understand that the whole rationale for gifted schools is based on the political pressure brought by middle-class parents, who always come out to vote. The result is that the "ungifted" children never get to read classics and are limited to ten-minute segments from minor works. Hispanic parents must not give credence to any political argument that claims that middle-class students are more gifted than poor students. Educational officials are always hard-pressed to describe what happens in these gifted classes. It appears to many critics that the classes are nothing more than an easy way to separate children by social or economic status or race.

The truth is that all ethnic groups and all economic groups

have gifted children. If the gifted classes turn out to be predominantly white and middle class, even though these groups are a minority in the school system, then it is clear that the gifted classes, which usually get extra financing and have the most qualified teachers, discriminate in practice.

Special Education

Programs for special education grew steadily in the decades after Congress passed a 1975 law guaranteeing educational equality for the handicapped. The system was administered under the terms of a 1980 consent decree issued by a federal judge in a class-action lawsuit filed on behalf of Jose P., a disabled Puerto Rican student. On orders of the court, the board has hired thousands of psychologists, educational evaluators, and other school employees to administer the special-education system. Because of its court protection, this bureaucracy continued to grow even as other parts of the school system were hit by budget cuts.

Several mayors and chancellors have since sought to reduce spending, without success. It had become obvious special ed needed extra scrutiny. The city was doing more than the law required to provide services to special education and bilingual students. I concluded that the Board of Education had allowed special-education and bilingual programs to develop bloated payrolls, and I began assembling a team of lawyers to study alternatives.

Out of the $8 billion allocated to the schools, $2 billion was being wasted in special education alone: 25 percent. Special education in New York City spread to numerous, meaningless categories: emotionally disturbed, language impaired, and a whole host of others.

Parents must do anything to avoid having their children placed in special education. Special education originally was intended for students with serious disabilities that would prevent them from learning in regular classrooms. These disabilities could be physical or emotional, but the act of Congress that established special education, for which I voted, required students to possess genuine handicaps. Of course there are such students. In practice, however, special education has become a dumping ground for troublesome or disruptive children, who may need slightly smaller classes or more attention but do not require the massive daily assistance special education is intended to provide. The evidence shows that very few of these children ever escape special education, and their performance is so poor that they are rarely even tested.

For practical purposes, special education is a dead end for Hispanic children, and no parent should agree to such designation for his or her son or daughter. Every finding that a child needs special education should be challenged, even if it is certified by a school psychologist. Those certifications are almost automatic and can easily be reversed. Many children are placed in special education because they are far behind in reading or writing, which is not by itself a proper criterion for condemning a child to this academic low road.

Moreover, special education is enormously expensive and reduces the amount of money available for regular education in a substantial way; in 1994 its vast costs cut the effective budget for students in regular education to $4,287 per pupil. Clearly, millions of dollars were (and still are) spent on special education without any visible results for most students in the program.

The points listed above are only a few of the policies educators implement that impede sound education. That is why I have argued for years that education cannot be left to educators, and that education is a full-time responsibility of the Hispanic community. It is not acceptable to say that the challenge of ensuring a sound education for Hispanic children is insurmountable. It is up to Hispanics to demolish these roadblocks to a sound, basic education. The issue is not, as many argue, a lack of money for the public-school system. If politicians parachuted more money into schools that pursued the policies outlined above, Hispanic children would remain uneducated. Educators developed these destructive policies; no one should expect those same educators to undo their own corrosive handiwork.

One possible policy remedy for this state of affairs would be mandatory standardized testing. I have heard, time and again, arguments that national standardized tests are biased because students from some minority groups sometimes perform less well on them. Those who make such claims are ignoring the factors that are responsible for poor test performance—namely, the poor quality of education received by many minority students in public high schools. That these students perform less well on national standardized tests should be seen as an indictment of the schools, not of exams that measure students' preparation.[7]

State boards of education and legislatures across the country are increasingly mandating such tests as a measure of what students have learned. Even progressive Massachusetts became, in 2003, one of twenty-six states that require students to pass at least one standardized test in order to graduate.

Parents, teachers, and students have rallied and railed against new standardized tests in Florida, Louisiana, Ohio, and Wisconsin, among other states. Some have taken their complaints to the courts, where they have argued that such tests discriminate against poor and minority children, as well as students in vocational and special-education programs. In 1999, under intense pressure from parents, Wisconsin officials repealed a requirement that students pass a new state test to graduate from high school.

Jake Levin, fifteen, a sophomore at Monument Mountain Regional High School in the northwest corner of Massachusetts, chose instead to vent his fury at the high-stakes tests sweeping the country. Levin is one of thirty-six sophomores in his school who skipped the test and one of at least three hundred statewide, according to interviews with principals and student organizers. He likened his protest to those against the Vietnam War.

The largest protest was at Cambridge Rindge and Latin School, where more than a hundred students boycotted the test, many of them assembling in the school auditorium for a teach-in that featured representatives of the American Civil Liberties Union and FairTest, an antitesting group. The protesters, who promised to boycott all eleven days of exams, described the tests as too long, too focused on memorization at the expense of critical thinking, and too pivotal, considering that it will soon be impossible to get a diploma without a passing grade.

Abigail Thernstrom, a member of the state Board of Education, said it was entirely appropriate for the state to erect one hurdle over which all students must jump. She said that the length of the tests, however onerous, gave students ample time to show their abilities and that it was not too much to ask every tenth-grader to be able to interpret a passage written on the level of Charles Dickens or to explain how to solve a geometry problem. "What we are asking for is knowledge that any student who wants a high-school diploma worth the paper it's written on should have," said Ms. Thernstrom, a senior fellow at the Manhattan Institute. "All other measures are subjective."

In an important about-face, the National Council of Teachers of Mathematics, the nation's most influential group of mathematics teachers, announced that it was recommending, in essence, that the arithmetic be put back into mathematics, urging teachers to emphasize the fundamentals of computation rather than focus on concepts and reasoning. The council added strong language to its then-current standards, established in 1989, emphasizing accuracy, efficiency, and basic skills like memorizing the multiplication tables. The message, said Joan Ferrini-Mundy, chairwoman of the committee to revise the standards, is "Get the right answer." For more than a decade, students as young as kindergartners have been encouraged to use calculators rather than computation; memorization, even of multiplication tables, has been spurned, and children have been given credit for arriving at reasonable rather than accurate answers, the implication being that there is no one right way of doing math. The council's documents have urged this approach as a better way of teaching minority students, female students, and others perceived as disadvantaged or afraid of math. California was the first state to embrace the 1989 standards and has also been at the center of the parental backlash against them. California recently introduced highly specific math standards for each grade, specifying, for instance, that children in fifth grade should be able to add, subtract, multiply and divide with decimals, and multiply and divide fractions.

A plan implemented in April 2000, in Texas and other states, would automatically admit the top 10 to 15 percent of graduates from high school into the public universities. But that remains, in the end, merely another form of social promotion: It fails to take into account the poor quality of public schools. If a college admits the top 15 percent of a school in which social promotion has been implemented, those students almost certainly will be underprepared. Their ranking in the school doesn't say anything about how well they can compute, spell, read, and write. High-school grades are meaningful only when the quality of the high-school curriculum is meaningful. In a move intended to increase local control of education and improve student performance, the sprawling Los Angeles Unified School District voted to reorganize itself into eleven semiautonomous subdistricts, each with its own superintendent, as part of a broader effort to head off more radical proposals for breaking up the nation's second-largest public-school system. The reorganization was proposed by the district's interim superintendent, Ramon Cortines. The plan calls for shrinking the district's two-thousand-person central office by more than eight hundred positions and transferring many of these employees to the new local districts, each with fifty to seventy-five schools. The Los Angeles schools have been plagued by a variety of problems, including severe crowding, dismal test scores, disputes over bilingual education, and polls showing a widespread lack of public confidence. The teachers' union, predictably, sought a 21 percent raise and bitterly opposed merit pay.

The education establishment's activities, in short, have undermined the interests of students, especially minority students. This has been the sad case not only in primary and secondary schools but in colleges and universities as well. No single story better encapsulates these failures of higher education than the decline of the City University of New York.

7

The Harvard of the Poor

WHEN GOVERNOR MARIO M. CUOMO appointed me to be a trustee of the City University of New York on June 30, 1990, I had no idea that educational standards in policy would turn out to be such highly politicized issues. Nor did I appreciate the extent to which the politics of education would become such a divisive issue in public discourse as it became apparent that the educational system was failing in every grade—from kindergarten through elementary and secondary schools and on to college.

CUNY's long slide into mediocrity began at six-thirty on a rainy spring morning in 1969. More than two hundred black and Puerto Rican students padlocked the gates of the south campus at City College and took over seventeen buildings to force the college to accept more minority students.

The protesters charged CUNY with racism and elitism, and demanded that it begin enrolling black and Puerto Rican students on a random basis until their representation on campus mirrored that of the city at large. Black and Hispanic students rioted at City College (CCNY) and took over the main building. They demanded an immediate change of admissions policy: that the same proportion of black and Hispanic students enrolled in the New York City high schools be accepted into the colleges of the City University, regardless of accomplishments. The city's liberal elite insisted these student demands would destroy CUNY, while minority leaders denounced standards as racist in themselves. And, with John Lindsay and other political leaders fearful of a major campus explosion in Harlem just two years after a summer of violent racial disturbances there, they succeeded in pushing City College and the City University of New York to open their doors to thousands of black, Hispanic, and even white students who earlier would not have qualified for admission.

A CUNY diploma had been an extraordinarily prestigious document since City College first opened as the Free Academy in 1847. Nicknamed "the Harvard of the Poor" (in fact, it once had *more* selective standards than Harvard), CUNY enabled generations of immigrants and low-income students to rise into the middle and upper classes.

CUNY alumni—writers, scholars, educators, actors, lawyers, CEOs, and physicians, among others—played starring roles in every field of human endeavor. Over the years CUNY produced eleven Nobel laureates—more than any other public university. Jonas Salk (City College '43) developed the polio vaccine. Gertrude Elion (Hunter '37) created the first drug to fight leukemia. Ada Louise Huxtable (Hunter '41) won the first Pulitzer Prize for criticism. Former alumni included Senator Daniel Patrick Moynihan, Congresswoman Shirley Chisholm, Supreme Court Justice Felix Frankfurter, civil-rights leader A. Philip Randolph, and me (City College '51). A. M. Rosenthal, who became executive editor of the *New York Times*, wrote, "My City College was an intellectually and academically elite school attended by students with family income ranging from not much to very not much."

My credentials as a magna cum laude graduate of City College were considered outstanding because I had successfully competed against some of America's best students. CUNY's admissions standards were very high, and only New York's top students could meet them. When open admissions came into effect, the university's biggest problem was in the quality of graduates turned out by New York City's public schools. Most students entering the university from the city's public schools could not pass the simple placement tests to take college-level classes and needed to take remedial classes in reading, writing, and math.

In fact, because of this systemic failure of the New York City public-school system, it became necessary for CUNY to serve largely as a clearinghouse for remediation.[1]

The difficulty in providing remedial education lies primarily in motivating students, in teaching skills that many students failed to learn in their high-school years, and in teaching students how to think critically and analytically.[2] It doesn't help the students if they have to take high-school work in college, at the same time they're taking college work. But, some might object, what can you do with the millions of students who enter college each year unprepared for college-level work? Why not try not admitting them to college?

CUNY had, under open admissions, a higher proportion of students who needed remedial classes than did most institutions around the country.[3] James Traub, author of *City on a Hill*,[4] performed a simple experiment at CUNY. Pretending to be a student, he spent an entire year in a remedial class at City College and found that the professor passed all the students who remained, even though they couldn't read or write. The professor claimed to feel sorry for them.

From a practical point of view, the desperate state of New York's public schools meant that many black or Puerto Rican students were in serious need of remediation: The achievement levels in poor neighborhoods were the lowest. Congresswoman Shirley Chisholm, Julius CC Edelstein, and I had introduced a program in 1966 known as SEEK (Search for Education, Elevation and Knowledge) in order to meet this need. By 1969, this alternative program for admission was beginning to attract more and better black and Hispanic applicants.

The students who conducted the strike in 1969 were not satisfied with the SEEK program. They demanded that all entry requirements be scrapped and that students be admitted to the City University on the basis of a high-school diploma. This was called "open admissions" and, if accepted, would completely change the character of the City University, since most high-school diplomas in black and Hispanic areas barely certified an ability to read and write. Certainly they did not prepare students for college.

The City College strike escalated in intensity and approached a riot. The debate about what to do engulfed the whole city. Chancellor Albert Bowker, the head of the City University, caved in to the demonstrators. So did Mayor Lindsay. He feared a major riot. Most public officials and all black and Hispanic leaders, except me, agreed with the mayor. I said that open admissions without standards would destroy the value of a City University diploma and would cripple the best institution in the city. Nevertheless, the new laid-back policy was approved.

As I predicted, the City University spiraled downhill, and

the value of its diploma plummeted. It took me thirty years and a fierce citywide battle to reverse the open-admissions policy.

CUNY's proud history, for political reasons, was destroyed by open admissions. CUNY dismantled its entrance requirements and admitted unprepared students who were given whatever remedial training they needed to participate in traditional college classes.

The agitation for change in admission policy grew out of a realization that CUNY's top four-year colleges remained overwhelmingly white even as the city around them was inhabited by growing numbers of black and Hispanic families.

I was the only public official who opposed open admissions in 1969. I felt that lowering standards would reduce the value of a City College diploma and close the door of opportunity to the poor of future generations.

Because of open admissions, many unprepared students would have to be hastily shuttled into remedial courses, which could stretch on for years. At some campuses such remedial offerings were disguised by names such as "developmental and compensatory courses." But the results were the same: Students were spending too much time acquiring skills that they should have learned in high school. In addition to providing a college education, in other words, CUNY's mission now included preparing students for college on an unprecedented scale.[5]

Proponents of open admissions at the time insisted that the

remedial students would be brought up to the level of the university's high standards. Instead academic standards dropped toward the level of the new students.[6] Yet the race to the bottom had only begun. When the new policies failed to bring in a satisfactory number of minorities, some senior colleges, motivated by the additional funding they received for admitting remedial students, petitioned for and won the right to enroll students from the lower half of their high-school class.

CUNY began a long decline. City College, having achieved the greatest prominence, had the greatest distance to fall—and fall it did, shattering its reputation as "the Harvard of the Poor" almost overnight. Only Queens College was able to maintain its academic caliber—a fact that led, predictably, to charges of "elitism."[7] The decline of standards led to a corresponding decline of institutional prestige.

The original idea was that students without college-level skills would remain in a sort of antechamber until they were up to speed. But this separation came under fire as "stigmatizing," so the walls between remedial and college-level courses came down.[8] Keeping remedial students out of regular courses was also decried as stigmatizing. Students who lacked reading and writing skills were usually allowed to take regular courses at the same time as remedial ones. As a result the distinctions between remedial and regular classes blurred.

Within months City College alone created 105 sections of remedial English and hired twenty-one full-time faculty members to teach them. Whereas 70 percent of its English classes had been literature courses, now 70 percent were remedial. Nearly nine in ten City College students required remedial writing instruction. Professors found themselves facing students who had never read a book, some of whom had no experience with written language or standard English.

Open admissions had a number of other unintended consequences. One of them was that huge cost—$35.5 million in its first year alone—which caused CUNY's budget to shoot up by 53 percent. Instead of concentrating on the students who could be helped, CUNY created ever lower levels of remediation for those who couldn't. To justify their labors, professors in such classes embraced a therapeutic mission. "The focus in lower remedial classes is as much, if not more, on the reader as the reading," said Rose Ortiz, developmental reading and writing coordinator at Staten Island. The objective, she explained, was to "become a more self-aware reader."[9] Another, and far more serious consequence, was that the new policy of reaching out to black and Hispanic students—regardless of grades and test scores—demoralized better-prepared students, resulting in white flight and in so-called ABC—Anywhere But CUNY—college shopping among gifted black and Hispanic students. In other words, precisely the opposite of what the student strikers had intended.

Childhood in Puerto Rico.
Left to right: my aunt Carmen,
me, my uncle Ubaldo, and my
aunt Ana.

My first grade-class in Caguas. I'm third from the right,
kneeling, in the front row.

My first political club, in East Harlem, 1960. I'm holding the microphone; Eleanor Roosevelt, first lady of modern American liberalism, is standing to my right. We were campaigning for John F. Kennedy for president.

Shaking hands with Mayor Robert Wagner, who appointed me commissioner of the Department of Relocation. I became the first commissioner of Hispanic orgin in New York City history.

Campaigning with Bobby Kennedy in the South Bronx during his Senate run, 1964. Bobby was the man who first brought me into politics on the national level, recruiting me to campaign for his brother in 1960.

Running for Bronx borough president, 1965. Daniel Patrick Moynihan is introducing me. Moynihan was another pol who would eventually bid good-bye to liberal orthodoxy on race and national security.

Meeting Luis Muñoz Marín, the famed governor of Puerto Rico, with Mayor John Lindsay at right, 1966. Muñoz Marín developed Operation Bootstrap, the battery of reforms that revitalized Puerto Rico's economy.

Campaigning for mayor with Manhattan borough president Percy Sutton, 1969.

Marching in the Puerto Rican Day Parade in New York, 1970.

Campaigning for Congress with Shirley Chisholm, 1970. Chisholm was one of the most forceful and memorable personalities in New York politics.

Another Puerto Rican Day Parade—in 1972, after I successfully ran for Congress. *Left:* Bella Abzug; *right:* Geraldo Rivera. Abzug was another unforgettable character in the political life of New York City.

Talking about the South Bronx with Jimmy Carter in the Oval Office, 1978.

Doing a handstand, 1978.

Left to right: Rudy Giuliani; my wife, Gail; me; and Donna Hanover Giuliani at Gail's and my wedding, 1996.

Rudy and me at my surprise seventieth birthday party, given for me by Gail.

Discussing the presidential campaign with George W. Bush on Long Island, 2004. (I've been a full-fledged Republican since 1998.) He followed my advice about aggressively pursuing the Hispanic vote and took 44 percent of it on Election Day.

Twenty-five years after its abdication of standards, not much ladder climbing went on at CUNY.

There remained good students and good programs throughout the system, but it was harder and harder for those students to get the education they deserved, because CUNY's remedial functions were swallowing up all others. While CUNY poured money into remediation, the rest of the university was being decimated by budget cuts. Library budgets had been sharply slashed, forcing the curtailment of hours and acquisitions. Like a compulsive gambler, CUNY continued to direct a disproportionate share of its resources to students with the least chance of success, while academically prepared students were largely left to fend for themselves.

When I was appointed to its board of trustees, CUNY had 200,000 degree-seeking students and 150,000 adult and continuing education students. It comprised ten senior colleges, six community colleges, a graduate school, a law school, a technical school, and an affiliated college of medicine. The campuses were situated throughout the five boroughs, and the students were mostly blacks and Latinos from poor families, many of whom arrived academically unprepared for college work. However, nobody talked about the broad-scale remediation that absorbed a large part of the course schedule and plenty of the system's budget.

My opposition to open admissions was well known to my fellow trustees, but I had little support for changes to the status quo. There are sixteen trustees on the board—ten appointed by the governor and five by the mayor, plus a student trustee. Many of the votes went 15–1, with me being the sole opposition. (There is also a nonvoting faculty trustee.)

In 1994, Rudolph Giuliani became mayor of New York City with my strong support. He immediately made it clear that he supported restoring standards at CUNY, and he appointed trustees who advocated my viewpoint.

This was a tumultuous time for CUNY. A black studies department had come into being at CCNY, as at other campuses across the country, in the early 1970s, in response to widely expressed feelings that the history of black people and their accomplishments had long been neglected.

But in 1991, three years before Giuliani's election, a huge storm of public controversy erupted around the chairman of City College's Department of Afro-American Studies, Dr. Leonard Jeffries, after he addressed a black cultural festival in Albany. Jeffries alleged a "systematic, unrelenting" attack from "the Jewish community" against himself and other black scholars and spoke of "a conspiracy, planned and plotted and programmed out of Hollywood" by Jews and Italians to denigrate blacks in films.

One of Jeffries's main political tenets was the genetic and social difference between the humanitarian and communal "sun people" of Africa and the "ice people" of Europe, where harsh conditions produced a culture of "domination, destruction and death"; Jeffries also said that Jews had helped to finance the slave trade. He went so far as to distribute booklets in class suggesting that the melanin in skin pigment may give blacks an intellectual advantage.

I was the only member of CUNY's board of trustees who was willing to say publicly that I planned to vote to oust the professor. The trustees leading the effort to get rid of Jeffries declined to name the others on their side. They did, however, identify Stanley Fink, a former Speaker of the New York Assembly, as an important swing vote. Fink declined to comment on the matter.

I said that I would vote to strip the professor of his chairmanship, because I had read Dr. Jeffries's remarks and there was no way I could possibly justify voting for him.

Jeffries, luckily, was replaced, on July 1, 1992; the vote by CUNY trustees represented an attempt to restore calm to a troubled department. Jeffries hyperbolically called his removal "an academic lynching and a media lynching."

The failure to meet ever-lowering standards, of which the Jeffries phenomenon was a consequence, needed to be explained away, so many strange theories popped up, just as they did later on other campuses. One theory was that critical, demanding teachers were guilty of trying to impose alien standards on minority cultures they didn't understand.

Leftist academics wanted to do away with the very distinction between academic proficiency and deficiency and replace it with the concept of "competence in one's own culture." Writing teachers in CUNY's English department argued that "deficiency" and "remediation" were mere "social constructs" designed to marginalize unwanted groups of people. Teachers were admonished to evaluate student writing "holistically" instead of "overcorrecting" prose. The new pedagogy promoted a "nonhierarchical," "collaborative," and "nonjudgmental" classroom. Professors were willing to evaluate writing on the basis of "creativity" and "sense of humor" rather than according to "mere" rules. As Geraldine de Luca, director of freshman English at Brooklyn College, said, "Even the concept of 'error' is beginning to feel repugnant to me." But employers were unlikely to be so empathetic. Yolanda Moses, then president of CUNY, had written that American universities were "products of Western society in which masculine values like an orientation toward achievement and objectivity are valued over cooperation, connectedness and subjectivity." This was the antiachievement message carried nationally by professors who stressed feelings and adjustment instead of learning. A primary example of this species of academic was J. F. Watts, chairman of the history department. His department placed a heavy leftist emphasis on "race, class, and gender" in courses on African labor history, decolonization, modern imperialism, U.S. labor history, slavery in colonial America, Latin American women, and modern Brazil. Few courses avoided smothering students in a stale mixture of revolutionary ideologies and ethnocentrism.[10] At the instigation of Professor Watts, the City College Faculty Senate's March meeting, attended by only thirty of its fifty-nine elected members, resolved unanimously to demand my resignation over the Jeffries affair. I was accused of "misusing" my position, "to discredit the university's historic mission and defame the achievements of its current students and recent graduates with a campaign of distortion, misinformation, half-truths and untruths." In particular I had "chosen to be the adversary rather than the advocate of the children of the whole people."[11] An adversary of the whole people? Not even the Chinese Politburo used that kind of Marxist jargon anymore—but such was the language in which these time-warped academics deconstructed the world. They wanted to put me on trial, essentially, as a "counter-revolutionary."[12]

In 1995, George Pataki became governor. He also began to change CUNY's board of trustees. By February 1997, Pataki had appointed Anne A. Paolucci, an English professor at St. John's University, as CUNY board chairman. Pataki had a unique opportunity to reshape the seventeen-member CUNY board of trustees. Key were his selections for a new chairman and vice chairman to provide firm leadership. Rudy Giuliani nominated three candidates, all advocates of restoring forgotten standards.

After Pataki named Paolucci as CUNY board chairman, he appointed me as vice chairman. He wanted us to reexamine some of the assumptions underlying CUNY and bring in fresh thinking to the system's twenty-one campuses.

Until then I was just a miscellaneous trustee, and I was generally in dissent. I was the 1 in the 15–1 votes. But with the five new Pataki and five new Giuliani appointees on the seventeen-member board, I became the voice of the majority. He asked the board to evaluate CUNY's mission and offer new ideas.

In May 1997, I received a call from a *New York Daily News* reporter telling me that some students were rioting at Hostos Community College in the Bronx, a bilingual campus that I had started in 1969. I learned that the students were rioting because they had failed a written assessment test that was a graduation requirement. They demanded that they receive their degrees even if they failed this test.

I called a special CUNY board meeting and confronted the president of Hostos College. She admitted that she had developed her own written assessment test, which was weaker than the one required by the university system. CUNY chancellor Ann Reynolds insisted that Hostos was the only college that administered a different test. The board of trustees, at my behest, passed a resolution requiring Hostos students to pass a written assessment test before they could graduate. This was a very modest English test, but only 13 of 104 passed it—87.5 percent failed. This signaled to the public and to me that Hostos was granting diplomas to students who did not know English. I said, "If you can't express yourself in English, you shouldn't graduate."

Worst of all, we discovered that Chancellor Reynolds had misled us when she claimed that Hostos was the only community college that did not require the English proficiency test; the other community colleges did not require it either. I was stunned that the other community-college presidents sat through the board of trustees meeting in which I questioned Hostos's president, Isaura Santiago, about her failure to require the proficiency test, and none of them admitted that they did not require it either. I criticized Reynolds, chancellor of CUNY's twenty-one-campus system, for tolerating grade inflation, failing to alert us trustees to important campus problems, and creating an intimidating environment that made college presidents unwilling to keep us informed.

On the issue of grade inflation, I discovered that even with the high percentage of students receiving remediation, most of them received A's and B's. When I discussed this with Dr. Reynolds, she said, "The same is true at Harvard." I told her that most CUNY students would not get into Harvard. The result of our discussions was that Chancellor Reynolds announced her departure for the presidency of the University of Alabama at Birmingham. Dr. Santiago soon resigned as president of Hostos Community College. Dr. Christopher Kimmick, provost of Brooklyn College, was appointed interim chancellor, and Dr. Dolores Fernandez was appointed president of Hostos Community College.

The Hostos scandal prompted a review of everything at CUNY. The Board of Trustees appointed me chairman of a committee to measure remediation's role in CUNY's operations. I discovered that this was impossible: There were so many euphemisms for remediation, such as "compensatory" or "progressive" education, that I could not fully plumb the depths of CUNY's remedial course offerings. I even found that in some colleges students received full college credit for remedial courses.

Finally, on May 6, 1998, Giuliani, who had lost patience with CUNY, appointed a task force to probe the university by executive order. "If we are promising a college education, we should deliver one," he told reporters. "We should stop playing make-believe. We have a lot of people at CUNY who were given high-school diplomas that aren't worth the paper they're written on."[13]

The task force was directed to examine:

1. CUNY's use of city funds
2. Open admissions and remedial education at CUNY

3. The possibility of arranging for third parties to provide remediation services to prospective CUNY students

4. The implementation of appropriate reform measures

The task force was headed by Benno C. Schmidt Jr., a former president of Yale University. It included yours truly; Heather MacDonald, a fellow at the Manhattan Institute, who had written critical reports on CUNY's remediation program; former state senator Manfred Ohrenstein; Jacqueline V. Brady, a vice president at Nomura Securities, International, Inc.; Richard T. Roberts, commissioner of the city's Department of Housing Preservation and Development; and Richard Schwartz, a special assistant to Giuliani.

Over the course of a year, we met at least twice a month. We visited every CUNY campus and interviewed many students, professors, administrators, and others. We held several public hearings that were marked by protests. Schmidt raised over six hundred thousand dollars to finance our consulting work. We prepared multiple drafts of our final report, and Schmidt and I discussed and revised crucial portions nightly.

Schmidt saw our task force as an opportunity to develop not just a new vision for the City University but a new paradigm for public higher education in America.

"At the eve of a new century, the United States urgently needs a model of a public university, and CUNY should be that model of excellence," Schmidt said. "CUNY has the chance to be the model for great public urban universities for the next century, and it's absolutely vital to make it right."[14]

We released our final report, *The City University of New York: An Institution Adrift,* on June 7, 1999. It contained not only 109 pages of observations and conclusions but also exhaustive documentation supporting all of our findings.

The report documented in incredible detail the massive extent of remediation at CUNY—87 percent of community-college freshmen and 72 percent of senior-college freshmen failed one or more of CUNY's remediation placement tests, and 55 percent of CUNY freshmen failed more than one. These tests merely measured whether incoming CUNY students could read or write English or understand math at low- to mid-high-school levels. The report noted that thirty years after open admissions, CUNY had not yet established valid and reliable remediation tests. We further concluded that if remediation is not effective and underprepared students proceed into college-level courses, the costs would be substantial, including:

- students who confront life without basic skills
- the waste of unprepared students' time in classes that are incomprehensible
- poor use of students' time, to the extent that courses are watered down

- the distraction of professors from college-level teaching
- the consequent erosion of standards

The report explained that for the previous decade the four-year graduation rate at CUNY's senior colleges hovered between 6 percent and 7 percent. CUNY's six-year graduation rate, roughly 30 percent, was still only about half of that in the State University of New York (SUNY) system (approximately 60 percent). With respect to associate degrees, we found that only about 1 percent of associate-degree entrants graduated in two years as expected. About 17 percent graduated within four years, compared to roughly 35 percent for SUNY. Clearly, graduation rates were abysmally low, with substantial costs to students, the university, and taxpayers. Similarly, on professional and licensing exams such as for nursing and teaching, CUNY's graduates underperformed state and national averages.

The report's recommendations included:

- reinventing open admissions to locate responsibility for remediation at the community-college level and ensuring that CUNY's senior colleges admit only those students who are prepared to succeed at college-level work
- instituting student-assessment testing that is consistent with modern assessment science

- recognizing remediation for what it is—an unfortunate necessity, thrust upon CUNY by the public-school system's failure, and a distraction from the university's main business
- establishing clear, objective standards for admission to and graduation from all degree programs

The reaction to the report was volcanic and predictable, especially because prior to its release I had introduced a broad resolution to eliminate remedial courses at CUNY's senior colleges. I argued that students should not be admitted to senior colleges unless they could do college work; remediation should be limited to community colleges. A legion of critics, including faculty members, public officials, editorial boards, and hundreds of demonstrators, could not challenge the report's findings because they were so thoroughly documented. So these naysayers resorted to predicting disaster if my resolution were approved.

They also stooped to racial attacks. They presented what they called scholarly research forecasting that over 45 percent of blacks and Latinos would be prevented from entering senior colleges.

There was picketing, and there was turmoil. Some school officials predicted that the new rule would slash enrollment by 50 percent.[15] Administrators had given exaggerated data about enrollment cuts to reporters in hopes of torpedoing the policy. They were playing the race card, and it was an outrageous thing to do. CUNY administrators used every tactic possible to prevent the vote and create the most destructive atmosphere that could be presented.[16]

As we met for a vote on May 26, the trustees were under tremendous pressure to defeat the proposal. Our vote was conducted to the accompaniment of sidewalk demonstrations and conference-room protests. The conference room, located inside CUNY headquarters at East Eightieth Street in Manhattan, was packed with students, teachers, community members, and activists as months of political pressure culminated in the last item on the day's agenda. When the nine other items had been settled, Paolucci deferred to trustee John Morning to present the resolution that would throw the meeting into chaos for several hours. Members of the audience began to chant "Keep admissions open! Stop the war on CUNY!" For several minutes the green marble walls of the conference room reverberated with the angry shouts of those who hold CUNY close to their hearts. When Dr. Paolucci began to lose control of the meeting, she ordered that the chanters be removed. As they were escorted out by SAFE officers (the campus police), a low mumble became an overwhelming roar as the rest of the audience began to sing "We Shall Not Be Moved." For ten minutes the chair struggled to continue with the meeting, only to be defiantly interrupted. Dr. Paolucci ejected most members of the audience after a handful of students and faculty members began chanting "Stop the racism! Stop the bastards! Stop the war on CUNY!" Fourteen people were arrested—including State Assemblyman Edward C. Sullivan, chairman of the assembly's Higher Education Committee—and given summonses for disorderly conduct when they would not move from a street outside CUNY headquarters.[17]

When order was finally restored, I quickly stepped in and introduced my plan to phase out remedial courses at four-year colleges by 2002. Applicants who failed one or more university tests in mathematics, reading, or writing would have to successfully complete a free summer program or pass remedial classes at a CUNY community college or elsewhere before being admitted to a four-year college. The transition would begin in September 1999 and would take three years, with Queens, Hunter, Baruch, and Brooklyn colleges the first senior colleges affected. Remedial education was kept intact, however, at CUNY's six community colleges. The changes would not apply to students who spoke English as a second language and who had received a high-school education abroad. After two hours of discussion came the moment of truth. In a slow and agonizing roll call, each member of the board voted for or against the substitution. When the votes were tallied, it was nine in favor, six against.[18] After a long struggle—which included demonstrations, pickets, and opposition from faculty, students, and public officials—I was successful in amending the Master Plan of the University so that no student could be matriculated at a senior college unless that student were ready for college work. My resolution was approved by the board of trustees—by one vote.

Any policy change required nine votes for passage. Going into the meeting, we'd had only eight. But I knew that Richard Stone, a law professor at Columbia University named to the board by Rudy, was wavering. Finally he declared that he would support the change. With that decision, which he called "one of the most difficult decisions I have ever made in my life," he became the ninth vote.[19] Stone said, "I would have preferred, perhaps, a true comprehensive plan. But I concluded, on the basis of very extensive discussions with other trustees, with governing authorities, and with many other people, that this was not to be—that the moment had indeed arrived to take a dramatic first step."

In the aftermath of the decision, several advocacy groups, including the Puerto Rican Legal Defense Fund, the Asian-American Legal Defense Fund, the NAACP Legal Defense Fund, and the American Jewish Congress, held strategy sessions and were contemplating a lawsuit. They considered alleging that the new policy violated Title VI of the Civil Rights Act, which said that entities that receive federal money should not discriminate by race or ethnicity. But some civil-rights lawyers noted that a significant number of white students would also be excluded, which undercut the civil-rights argument.

Juan Figueroa, president and general counsel for the Puerto Rican Legal Defense Fund, which I helped found, was one of my severest critics. "This is nothing less than Proposition 209 dressed in the rhetoric of standards," he said, referring to the California initiative ending minority preferences. "What they're really talking about is eliminating affirmative action from the process and resegregating the system."

Professor Richard Wade, a historian at the Graduate Center who had no experience teaching remedial students, called open admissions the linchpin of the city.

"If we didn't have a university that will take care of the people, what will they do?" Wade asked. "I wouldn't want to be here if there was [sic] no CUNY. We'd have to build a lot more jails."

Congressman Charles Rangel also invoked the false dichotomy of college versus jail, as did others. The *Amsterdam News* editorialized that the creation of two separate-but-unequal school systems would turn CUNY into "Apartheid University." *New York Times* columnist Bob Herbert said Giuliani was waging an "unnecessary and unconscionable war on the weak and the poor and the black and the brown," who were, according to Herbert, "kids whom many would like to see cleansed not only from CUNY's landscape but as much as possible from the very consciousness of privileged New Yorkers."

The chairwoman of the City Council's Committee on Higher Education accused Benno Schmidt and me of ethnic cleansing. I replied that I had no intention of bringing white students from Kosovo to attend CUNY; if I proposed standards for CUNY, it was for the benefit of black and Latino students who constitute a majority of the student body and would attend in even larger numbers in future years.

I became a Republican in June 1998, after I was accused of being a tool of Pataki and Giuliani, both of whom were Republicans. I said at the time that I did not know that believing in standards was a Republican idea, but if so, I would join the Republican Party. Shortly before the task-force report was released, Dr. Paolucci resigned as chairwoman of CUNY's board of trustees, and Governor Pataki appointed me chairman on June 1, 1999.

This was obviously a time of enormous ferment for CUNY. I would be able to fill many top positions that were open at the university and its undergraduate colleges.

Giuliani said that my task should be "changing a culture of total failure. It's changing a culture that embraces a one-percent graduation rate and tries to defend it, excuse it, and alibi for it as opposed to dramatically trying to change it. He has got to have everyone take a leap of faith toward high standards."

I was in a unique position to press for the task force's recommendations. To me the goals outlined in the report would serve as the university's "goalposts."[20]

My first priority was to select a strong chancellor who knew the City University and would be ready to work with the remediation policy and set high standards for the colleges. We needed to have a mayor and a governor and a board of trustees and a chancellor who were working together. Without these we would never have a meaningful plan for reform.[21]

I also rejected the idea that reducing funds has contributed to the ills of community colleges. If there's no test to determine whether students have finished remediation, more money can't and won't solve the problem.

On July 23, I introduced a resolution to appoint Matthew Goldstein, who had served previously as president of Baruch College, as CUNY's permanent chancellor. I asked the trustees to waive a search for a new chancellor on the grounds that the university needed a strong leader who was an unapologetic supporter of higher admission standards, which Dr. Goldstein surely was. The trustees agreed, and Dr. Goldstein was approved.

After much turmoil the board of trustees approved the resolution to eliminate open admissions. The next step was to secure the approval of the Board of Regents, the state's top educational oversight institution. By this time I was well aware that educational issues are political in nature. Therefore, I made sure to meet with the state's legislative leaders, particularly Senate Majority Leader Joseph Bruno, a Republican, and Assembly Speaker Sheldon Silver, a Democrat. Speaker Silver's support was especially crucial, because by some strange quirk of state law the governor does not appoint the Board of Regents. The state assembly, controlled by its Speaker, makes those decisions. Both Senator Bruno and Speaker Silver were gracious and supportive.

After the Board of Regents approved my resolution, none of my critics' dire predictions came true. The opposite was the case. Students have met the new standards. As I argued all along, if a CUNY college degree represents genuine effort and scholarship, it will be more valuable to students in the long run. In fall of 2000, freshman enrollment rose 3.3 percent, recruitment of transfer students showed an increase of 6.5 percent, and the ethnic component of the student body remained virtually constant. New York City public-school graduates, recent immigrants, and adults were returning to CUNY to seek meaningful ways to better their lives. When we changed the standards to require a test to enter the senior colleges, many of the students who failed took remedial courses in the summertime. Of roughly seventeen thousand pre-freshmen who made this special effort to attend summer skills programs, most succeeded and then enrolled.

But the jewel in the crown of CUNY reform was unquestionably the new honors program. For these hundred slots available in the program, over a thousand students applied. The typical test score for those applicants was roughly 94 percent, and their SAT scores averaged 1300 out of a possible 1600. (It's important to distinguish this from the practice of tracking I mentioned earlier—this program is based on a record of quantifiable scores and grades, not race.) This further demonstrates that high expectations bring results. If we raise standards, students will work harder to satisfy them.

On June 5, 2001, I resigned as chairman of the board of trustees of CUNY in order to run for mayor of New York City. But I will always remain proud of my role in restoring standards to the City University, which now is truly "A University on the Move."

From the vantage point of thirty years, it can be said that CUNY's central failure was that it let protesters define a college degree as a good that whites were withholding from minority groups, a good that could be extracted by political pressure. If the Board of Trustees and the administration had insisted, from the outset, that a degree came only from hard work and learning, the history of CUNY might have been very different.

But what happened to CUNY was an extreme manifestation of a nationwide trend in education over the last quarter of the twentieth century. The idea of the university underwent a radical transformation in the 1960s. As unrest tore through American cities, higher education came to be seen as a means for defusing the nation's social and racial crises. It was no longer enough for a college merely to educate; universities were called on to enfranchise minority groups through admissions and curricular changes.

American education devoted considerable energy to coming up with things other than education that it might be good at. Putting higher education into the service of racial peacekeeping was one of the most fateful of those experiments.

This was, in some sense, merely part of a larger, beneficial phenomenon: the GI Bill and the huge increase in college attendance it permitted. Paul Fussell described this phenomenon in his book *Class*—the sprouting up of new universities initially overnight, and new programs to fund them. Gradually college became less a stamp of the elite and more an economic good, a ticket to the middle class. It became, rather than an educational institution, a device for a broader kind of social promotion. As a result the value of a degree itself was vastly cheapened—and not only for minorities.

The argument for open admissions that seemed most compelling at the end of the 1960s—racial justice—is today the least persuasive. CUNY is no longer majority white, even though it no longer has open admissions. In 1992, blacks, Hispanics, and Asians constituted 63.1 percent and whites 36.9 percent of the total enrollment. Because of demographic change, argues Paula Fichtner of Brooklyn College, CUNY could go back to being an elite institution and still maintain its ethnic diversity.

This proves, in other words, that economically disadvantaged minorities can achieve just as much as middle-class whites, when just as much is asked of them.

Realizing that standards of excellence are a key to minority progress caused me to question many of my long-held liberal beliefs about what kinds of policies would best improve the lives of the disadvantaged. This epiphany, as I will recount in the next chapter, led me to join Rudolph Giuliani in his efforts to save the city of New York.

8

From Kennedy Democrat to Giuliani Republican

My political career, like my decision to pursue a serious education, was the result of a happy accident. After graduating from law school, as I mentioned earlier, I worked for several years as a tax lawyer. At that time, in the late 1950s, Emilio Nuñez was the only Hispanic judge in New York City. Through Judge Nuñez other criminal-court judges heard that I spoke Spanish. I was soon assigned to criminal cases on a pro bono basis. Although I was not paid, I accepted this work because I could get experience trying cases. I was also outraged that young people floundered behind bars because they were too poor to hire counsel, and neither government nor private charities provided them assistance.

My most important case involved an eighteen-year-old Puerto Rican who had been indicted for first-degree robbery—a felony. At that time it carried a mandatory sentence of ten to thirty years. He was accused of mugging an old man at night in a Queens housing project and taking a small sum of money from him, perhaps twenty-five or thirty dollars. This was a first-degree felony with a stiff mandatory sentence because it was committed *at night*. (If the crime had happened in the sunshine, it would have been less serious, even if thousands of dollars were involved.) We see the same legal disparities today, when top corporate CEOs steal millions of dollars and defraud stockholders yet are penalized more lightly than minor offenders who commit street crimes.

When I first met the defendant, he had been jailed for about a year. He spoke no English and was oblivious to the charge against him. When I questioned him, he said he did not know where he was on the night of the crime, so it was impossible for him to establish an alibi. I got copies of that night's weather report. Fortunately, it had rained that evening. I photographed the crime scene and determined that the nearest streetlight was about ninety feet away. The only testimony against my client was based on the positive identification provided by the old man who was mugged. The result was a hung jury. This was a major victory: No blacks or Latinos sat on the jury who could be said to sympathize with the defendant.

The judge was so outraged by the verdict that he called me to the bench and said, "Young man, I want you to know that I believe the defendant is guilty and the only reason there was a hung jury was because of the persuasiveness of counsel."

"Thank you, Judge," I replied. "I want you to know that this is the first case I've ever tried."

Turning pale, the judge asked me, "Do you realize that in such a serious case, if the defendant had been convicted, the conviction could be set aside, in a coram nobis proceeding, on the grounds that counsel was inexperienced?"

The judge ordered a new trial, but he assigned an experienced criminal lawyer from Queens to try the case with me. This time the young man was acquitted.

I tried many other criminal cases. Most of them reflected poorly on the criminal-justice system, the police, or the judiciary. I told Judge Nuñez that there had to be a better way to address the problems of the Puerto Rican community than on a case-by-case basis. By the time someone lands in jail, too much has already gone wrong. Social problems, I reasoned, ought to be addressed at the source. Nuñez suggested that I enter politics and join a political club. This proved to be a fateful piece of advice.

I returned to my old West Harlem neighborhood, which had become heavily Puerto Rican. I found a Democratic Club on 145th Street, where I met Angelo Simonetti, the district leader, and told him that I wanted to join. I told him I was a Puerto Rican lawyer, a CPA, and a good speaker thanks to my experience on the moot-court team in law school. I told him I was sure I'd be able to register many people in the area to vote, and I offered to pay my membership dues on the spot. He told me not to pay then but to wait until the club's annual meeting. He asked for my card so he could send me an invitation. That was in 1957—and I'm still waiting for it.

I visited other Democratic clubs and received the same reaction. I soon realized that the last thing any of these leaders wanted was an aggressive young Puerto Rican who could eventually take over their organization. So I went back to see Judge Nuñez.

He told me that there was only one place in Manhattan or in the whole city where there was a Puerto Rican district leader—in East Harlem. Tony Mendez ran the Caribe Democratic Club. Judge Nuñez assured me that I would be welcomed there.

He was right. Mendez and his wife, Isabel, were delighted to meet me. They introduced me to all the other members. The club met Mondays and Thursdays and welcomed a large number of Puerto Ricans from East Harlem and across the city. They showed up to air their problems with housing, welfare, health care, courts, and every kind of calamity imaginable. I learned to confront these issues by writing letters to city agencies or landlords and going to court when necessary. This made me an expert on constituent services.

I eagerly absorbed everything there was to know about running a political campaign. I registered voters, supervised petition drives, and learned all the tricks available to get candidates on and off the ballots. I learned to argue cases before the Board of Elections and in courts. I campaigned on sound trucks and in the subways. I met candidates for every office from assemblyman to governor. For example, when Averell Harriman ran for governor in 1958, he came to the club and I translated his speech into Spanish.

I also became the club's spokesman to the rest of the city. Tony Mendez frequently got calls requesting someone to speak at public events, such as at Town Hall on issues affecting the Puerto Rican community. He was always happy to send me, because I earned the club rave reviews. Word got around that there was an articulate Puerto Rican available to speak and debate on any subject. Democratic Party reformers were looking for just such a person. My political star began to rise.

By late 1959, I was ready to start my own political organization. That opportunity arrived at the beginning of 1960, when I got a call from Steve Smith, the husband of John Kennedy's sister Jean. He was looking for a Puerto Rican to head the campaign in East Harlem for the next president of the United States, John Fitzgerald Kennedy.

In 1960, JFK had the full support of the Regular Democratic Organization (RDO), headed by Carmine De Sapio. However,

JFK did not trust the RDO's regulars, because he knew that they never had been interested in turning out the black and Puerto Rican vote. He thought he needed those groups' support to carry New York State in the November election against Richard Nixon.

Kennedy launched a competing organization known as Citizens for Kennedy. It was headquartered at 277 Park Avenue, a mansion owned by his father, Joseph Sr., which was about to be demolished and replaced with an office building. His idea was to make sure that reformers, independent Democrats, blacks, and Latinos who were not part of the regular Democratic organization worked directly with the Kennedy campaign to get out the vote.

Team Kennedy was particularly interested in East Harlem because the number of registered voters was so low, and higher registration levels and increased turnout would benefit Kennedy. Someone told them about me, and soon my phone rang, summoning me to a meeting with JFK's high command.

I went to 277 Park and spoke with Bobby Kennedy, Steve Smith, and other top leaders of the Kennedy organization. Bobby Kennedy was the chairman of his brother's presidential campaign. He was very short-tempered with everyone on the campaign staff. He was a slight young man and had the famous Kennedy hair. He was pleased to meet me, and we agreed that I would open a "Kennedy for President" storefront at Third Avenue between 115th and 116th streets, a part of East Harlem that the RDO controlled. In that district Congressman Alfred E. Santangelo was the district leader, Frank Rosetti was the assemblyman, and John Merli was the councilman. Indeed, every elected official was of Italian descent, although the area's population long ago had become overwhelmingly Puerto Rican and black. Needless to say, few of these newcomers were registered to vote, and the rest were not encouraged to do so. My job was to register them and turn out the largest possible vote for John Kennedy that November.

In other words, I was sent to present a direct challenge to the RDO in its own territory. Although we all were Democrats, it was understood that an increase in Puerto Rican and black registration and votes would end the control of this area by Americans of Italian heritage. This would not happen without a major political fight.

I opened the storefront and hung a Kennedy for President placard in the window. I brought in an old desk and chairs and decorated the club with campaign posters. This was around April 1960, and the campaign organization had paid the rent through November. I got microphones and sound equipment and literature from the Kennedy camp. I installed signs in English and Spanish and opened the club to the public with a staff of only one person—me!

I stood by the door and told passersby that this was Kennedy for President Campaign Headquarters and that everyone was welcome to come in and help. Most people couldn't believe it, because no one had ever made them feel welcome in a political club in that district. But the Puerto Ricans and blacks who walked by were fascinated with Kennedy, and they loved the idea that they could help. They came into the clubhouse, gave me their names and addresses, and told me that they were not registered to vote. I told them I would get them registered and gave them literature to hand out to their friends and neighbors.

They asked me if Kennedy himself were coming to East Harlem. I said, "Of course, and so will other great political figures." Within a very short time, I built an organization and filled the storefront club with people throughout each day. One of my favorite pictures shows that wonder lady, Eleanor Roosevelt, standing beside me, surrounded by a group of Puerto Ricans who had come to the clubhouse to hear her speak.

Even more exciting, John Kennedy himself agreed to visit East Harlem. We scheduled a late-summer rally at 116th Street and Lexington Avenue. This was known in East Harlem as the "Lucky Corner" because former mayor Fiorello La Guardia and seven-term congressman Vito Marcantonio had held their closing campaign rallies on this very spot.

To everyone's surprise, some twenty thousand people showed up, and they crowded not just the Lucky Corner but every street for blocks around. Ironically, the wildest applause was not for Senator Kennedy but for his wife, Jackie, who was then pregnant with John Jr. She addressed us in fluent Spanish. The rally was a spectacular success.

The next step was the registration campaign. This was not easy, because in 1960 there was a literacy test in New York State, which everyone had to pass in order to register to vote. This literacy test was embedded in New York's state constitution in the 1920s, ironically to disenfranchise Italian immigrants.

Over the years the literacy requirement had become a device to keep blacks and Latinos from voting. I campaigned throughout East Harlem inside a sound truck urging people in both English and Spanish to register so they could vote for Kennedy for president.

The people of East Harlem responded with enthusiasm. During the registration period, long lines of Puerto Ricans and blacks formed in front of schools so they could take the literacy test and register. The RDO responded with its usual tactics. Schools magically ran out of the literacy test. Teachers suddenly became unavailable to administer the test. Registration inspectors crawled like slugs in hopes that registrants would tire of waiting and simply leave as they had arrived— unregistered.

I traveled from school to school to combat these delaying tactics. Fortunately, the Santangelo organization did not know who I was. Since I was tall and slim and spoke with authority wherever I went, it never occurred to Santangelo's captains that

I was their opponent. They thought I was a lawyer brought in from downtown to help out.

At one point I walked into a school at about four o'clock in the afternoon, and one of Santangelo's captains said to me, "You can't believe the garbage that's coming in here."

"What do you mean?" I asked.

He answered, "This guy Badillo is bringing in all these blacks and Puerto Ricans to register, and he's going to beat us. We've got to stop him."

"What do you have in mind?" I wondered.

"The school is supposed to stay open till ten-thirty P.M.," he said, "but I'm going to close up at nine o'clock, when the biggest crowd comes in."

I nodded. "Good idea."

Sure enough, promptly at nine, the school closed. I was waiting outside with a pad and pen. I jotted down as many names and addresses as I could, with details of how long people had waited in line. I drew up affidavits and a complaint and filed a lawsuit with the Board of Elections.

I persuaded fourteen Puerto Ricans to testify at the trial. As a result I won the case, and the complainants were allowed to register after the registration period had expired. It was a small victory because these were only fourteen people out of thousands who had been turned away throughout the district, but it had huge symbolic significance: That was the first time in New

York history that there had been legal proof of discrimination against blacks and Latinos by agents of the Board of Elections. Moreover, it gained me recognition as a serious and effective competitor.

When the enrollment period ended, it turned out that my district had boosted registration by 48 percent, the largest increase in the state! This despite the large numbers of people who were turned away because of our opponents' tactics. After this experience, it no longer could be said that poor people were uninterested in politics. It was obvious that they were being illegally denied full participation. In other words, New York City in that sense was not so different from the Jim Crow South.

When the November election finally arrived, Kennedy won an overwhelming victory in the district but was elected president with just 49.7 percent of the vote to Nixon's 49.5 percent, a difference of only 118,574 ballots. The Kennedy campaign's New York strategy was successful, however, and my future as a political leader was assured.

After this somewhat accidental beginning, I entered fully into the turbulent life of New York City politics. I became a housing commissioner appointed by Mayor Robert F. Wagner Jr. I was elected borough president of the Bronx when John Lindsay was mayor. I saw the damage his incompetence, and that of his successor, Abe Beame, inflicted on New York, economically and socially. I made a few runs at Gracie Mansion myself but was defeated, inevitably, by factional strife within the Democratic Party. Nonetheless I remained a loyal Democrat. But by the end of the 1980s, things had taken a serious turn for the worse. Crime was rampant; the schools were falling apart; unemployment had skyrocketed. Not even the Greenwich Village firebrand Ed Koch had been able to make any lasting difference. When he decided to run for a fourth term, in 1989, I knew it was a serious mistake.

First of all, voters frown upon four-term executives. Governor Nelson Rockefeller was a rare exception to that rule.

Second, Koch was plagued by scandals in his third term involving Donald Manes, the Queens borough president who fatally stuck a knife into his own heart while facing graft charges. Also, Stanley Simon, the Bronx borough president, resigned and went to jail for corruption.

More important, the city was in a slump. At the end of Koch's third term, the discontent over New York's declining quality of life—filthy and broken-down streets, poor housing, bad schools, run-down parks, graffiti-scarred and crime-ridden subways—made municipal services the main issue for many New Yorkers. The groups who were dissatisfied with Ed Koch in 1982 were even more dissatisfied with him in 1989, primarily because of the failure to provide essential services in the city. The deterioration of city services was a prime topic of local commentators. Nobody could blame the New York Jets for making an end run to New Jersey after five years of complaints about flooding toilets in Shea Stadium, humorist Russell Baker suggested. "What every New Yorker knows he means when uttering that ad man's cry is 'I love New York, even though it's a dump.'"

Consequently, to Koch's surprise, David Dinkins, Manhattan's black borough president, defeated him in the Democratic primary. Dinkins went on to beat the Republican Rudolph W. Giuliani by less than 2 percent of the vote. With the slimmest City Hall victory since 1905, Dinkins became New York's first black mayor. Shortly afterward, the city began to spin out of control.

I had endorsed Dinkins in the general election against Giuliani. A few days after Dinkins entered City Hall in January 1990, I called him and told him that as Koch's deputy mayor I had compiled a list of neighborhoods that were in danger of erupting in racial violence. We had developed a community-assistance unit to respond rapidly to any disturbance. I told Dinkins that the list included about thirty areas, from Manhattan to the Bronx. Dinkins thought reviewing these contingencies was a good idea and transferred me to his deputy mayor, Bill Lynch. My friend Tonio Burgos, who knew about these discussions, talked to Bill Lynch several times. But after a while Lynch stopped returning phone calls. Nothing happened.

Crown Heights, Brooklyn, was more or less equally divided between blacks and Jews. The latter were mainly Hasidim, a very conservative group of Orthodox Jews who wear modest dark clothing, sport long beards, and generally stick close together. Because they do not travel during the Sabbath and attend just a couple of specific synagogues, they tend to live very near to one another in this densely populated neighborhood. As a result this put the Hasidim in constant competition with blacks for apartment vacancies, which helped establish a sometimes tense relationship between these groups.

On the blistering night of August 19, 1991, a Hasidic family's car struck and killed a black child in that area. The incident quickly became racialized, and a riot broke out in Crown Heights. The Dinkins administration failed to respond appropriately. For three nights blacks committed bloody attacks against Hasidic Jews. Yankel Rosenbaum, an Australian Hasidic rabbinical student, was walking home during the rioting when a black youth named Lemrick Nelson, then sixteen, fatally stabbed him four times. Rosenbaum, it is disputed by no one, was killed purely because of his appearance, which marked him as a Jew. The failure of Dinkins and his police commissioner to take forceful action permitted a total breakdown of law and order. Many called this an anti-Semitic pogrom, America's worst since the nineteenth century.

A jury acquitted Lemrick Nelson of the murder of Yankel

Rosenbaum. Dinkins responded to the acquittal by announcing that we live in "a society requiring that we accept and abide by the jury system." Jews—not just Hasidim and conservatives— were outraged at Dinkins's tepid response. He showed no moral leadership; he placated constituencies. Jews reacted to the verdict with the suspicion that justice would never be served for this murder, and that's precisely where a mayor needs to step in—to calm and to demonstrate an understanding of the anger. But Dinkins said nothing to assure Jews at all. He deplored the murder but did little else. After the acquittal Nelson's lawyers celebrated at a dinner with some members of the jury. Dinkins said little about either of the events. Nor was he among the politicians who called for a federal investigation of the murder. One suspects that if David Dinkins gave Yankel Rosenbaum any thought, it was only to hope that Dinkins didn't have to hear Rosenbaum's name much between the murder and the next Election Day. Crown Heights was not only a racial problem, it was a crime—New York's largest in years—and a collapse of law enforcement in the face of crime. Historically, in Europe the police helped the pogroms. In Crown Heights officialdom allowed the pogrom to overwhelm or sideline the police. That is what scared so many New Yorkers—the breakdown of the law.

Dinkins failed to unite New Yorkers under "one standard." He had been unable or unwilling at these critical points to articulate a common standard of behavior for all New Yorkers—especially when doing so would jeopardize his political base in the black community. Because he is a black man, Dinkins could speak out against the abdication of standards. But he failed in the most important thing: to point out that in this city there has to be one standard for everyone, blacks, whites, and Latinos.

But it wasn't just that Dinkins appeared indecisive in crises, such as Crown Heights, or that he failed to support a policeman in a Washington Heights shooting. The city seemed ungovernable. Michael Tomasky wrote:

> More than 250,000 jobs lost to the city since Dinkins took office. More than 1 million New Yorkers are on welfare. The schools range from mediocre to disgraceful. The streets aren't safe. It's reckoned a good year when fewer than 2,000 people are murdered. His administration had been directionless, launching a handful of programs here and there, reversing itself on policies concerning the homeless, for example, and generally doing very little to give New Yorkers a sense that their city, where their daily lives get more difficult each year, is moving forward. The bureaucracies are immovable. The unions are intractable. Wall Street is imperious. The bond rates are skeptical. Nothing seems to get done.[1]

I remember a *New York Post* headline that screamed DAVE, DO SOMETHING!—a sentiment that truly reflected the popular mood. Indeed, it appeared the city was out of control, and no one seemed to know what to do.

To New Yorkers, decline seemed an incremental, inexorable process, as though the entire city were stuck on an escalator descending slowly from the penthouse to the basement. Since 1989, the number of AIDS cases in the city had more than doubled. Tuberculosis was up. The city's welfare population had rocketed past 1 million—a number that would make the New Yorkers on public relief the seventh-largest city in America. The economic strains inevitably widened social divisions. In Queens and Staten Island, two of the city's five boroughs, serious movements to secede were under way. In Manhattan, teenagers marched down Madison Avenue with T-shirts that commanded BACK THE F——— UP.

When you claim a higher moral ground, as progressives always do, you'd better stay up there. In such a milieu, knees jerk to the left as easily as to the right. Dinkins, and progressive New York in general, spoke only in the coded language of identity politics and entreaties to oppressed subgroups. It was language that sounded noble when talking of black or Latino "empowerment," cloaking itself in the rubrics of civil rights, comity, and love of fellow person, but in the end it was the same old interest-group palm greasing, just like the Irish politicos used to play it, dressed up in a multicultural tuxedo. It pretended to be something it was not. It dismissed as Neanderthals, as relics, those who did not buy into its precepts, implying they were somehow in the way (of what, it was not clear). The black mayor and the social movements that started in the 1960s and eventually lifted him into the city's highest office faced a referendum. His coalition—black and Latino activists and what were called, in PC shorthand, "progressive whites"—teetered on the brink of the identity-politics cliff. A new coalition—white outer-borough ethnics, newer immigrants, and people of color who weren't schooled in traditional liberalism and who increasingly distrust its postures and buzzwords—stood ready to supplant them.

Dinkins did not make things easier for himself. Critics piled on him, for instance, for remarks he made to a predominantly black radio audience. Stung by criticism from some Jews and other whites for failing to intervene earlier to quell violence in Crown Heights, Dinkins commented, "To your listeners, let me just say that I have been out in the street a lot. I've spoken to two Brooklyn churches—I guess yesterday or the day before. I was in Crotona Park yesterday. I am out in the street a lot, and I see a lot of brothers and sisters everywhere I go, and I got to tell you the reception I get, especially the children—and you know I love children—the reception I get is so wonderful and so encouraging and it sustains me. . . . And I don't care what other folks are saying. I have some faith and confidence in my own ability and what I have done. And when the brothers and sisters come out and encourage me, I want you to know it makes everything all right."

The Liberal Party leader Raymond B. Harding declared, "I, for one, am bone-weary of being considered as 'other folks.'" I cautioned, "Those leaders who remain silent at this moment in the city's history will ultimately have to account to the people for their failure to take a stand." Norman Siegel, head of the New York Civil Liberties Union, remarked that "your reference to the 'brothers and sisters' can only be construed as a reference to African-Americans. Your words have the tone of setting race against race, brother against brother, and sister against sister by suggesting that people choose sides of a moral issue and public policy debate on the flimsy and scurrilous basis of their skin color."

Dinkins's 1993 rematch with Giuliani was shaping up to be a mismatch. Dinkins's fire commissioner, the city's top Latino official, resigned, endorsed Giuliani, and accused unnamed city officials of bias against Latinos. Norman Adler, a political consultant, reflected, "David Dinkins's legitimate slogan should be: He wasn't crushed to a pulp."

I had entertained the idea of running for mayor against Dinkins in 1993 and even prepared a campaign button that said "One City, One Standard" to underscore that the divisions

Dinkins had allowed to grow could be eradicated. However, I thought it would be a very difficult campaign, because it would mean a Democratic Party primary challenge against an incumbent. That type of campaign seldom succeeds.

Meanwhile, my law partner, Raymond Harding, who was the de facto head of the Liberal Party, arranged for me to meet Rudy Giuliani for dinner at the Park Avenue apartment of another of my law partners, Richard Fischbein. I already had heard plenty about Giuliani. He had been a top Justice Department official under President Reagan. He later was appointed United States Attorney for the Southern District of New York. As a crusading prosecutor, he went after members of the Mafia as well as Wall Street tycoons accused of financial improprieties. Unlike most federal prosecutors, Giuliani often tried cases himself. He put away former Democratic congressman Mario Biaggi for extorting almost $2 million from a defense contractor, as well as Stanley Friedman, the former Bronx Democratic chief.

After his years in law enforcement, Giuliani pursued a career in electoral politics. He had lost to Dinkins barely in 1989 and had spent the next four years learning about issues and preparing to run for mayor in 1993 on the Republican and Liberal Party lines, the same ones on which he campaigned in 1989.

In addition to Giuliani and me and my law partners, Peter Powers, Giuliani's campaign manager, and David Garth, his television and press manager, also attended this meeting. We discussed the enormous challenges facing the city. I found Giuliani very well informed on nearly every issue. He was totally committed to change. For example, Giuliani was particularly determined to reduce crime. To that end he believed in the "broken windows" policing philosophy advanced by the Manhattan Institute for Public Policy Research and political scientists George Kelling and James Q. Wilson. This theory essentially says that leaving a building's broken windows unrepaired signals to criminals that no one cares, which in turn fuels even more crime. An increasing sense of disorder intimidates the law-abiding, who then tend to avoid the streets, further yielding the sidewalks to the lawless, in an ever-downward spiral.

Conversely, repairing those windows suggests that someone is in charge and someone cares, so criminals had better watch out. Fixing broken windows makes it less likely that hoodlums will attempt other, more serious crimes. Combating minor offenses such as graffiti, aggressive panhandling, and public urination, to name a few, makes purse snatching, robbery, rape, and murder less likely.

This idea capsized the liberal conventional wisdom—that the root cause of crime was poverty and that policing was largely irrelevant until incomes could be elevated in downtrodden areas. Rudy Giuliani and I rejected that view, which happened to be elitist, if not racist: It essentially equated poor people with criminals. We believed that better policing could remove and isolate lawbreakers while giving peaceful residents the sense that their neighborhoods were worth improving and the courage to help the police do so.

We all discussed the need to reverse Dinkins's policy of forbidding NYPD officers to arrest drug dealers on the streets and instead assigning special drug task forces to conduct arrests. Dinkins's excuse was that corrupt beat officers might alert drug dealers to impending sweeps. The trouble was that by the time the special task forces arrived, the drug dealers were gone. Our view was that while *some* policemen might be corrupt, *all* drug dealers are corrupt, and therefore every policeman should be able to make drug arrests.

Similarly, we agreed that auto thefts had skyrocketed because of the failure to enforce the law. I told Giuliani about a friend whose car was stolen. When he reported the theft at a police precinct, officers gave him a piece of paper to present to his insurance company. We recalled that when we attended law school, we learned that stealing a car was a felony that demanded prosecution, not a certificate for an insurance claim. Giuliani, as a former federal prosecutor, was particularly emphatic on this issue.

We also agreed that New York's welfare laws were not being enforced. Many welfare recipients who supposedly lived alone with children under age eighteen in fact resided with working individuals. That disqualified them from welfare. Despite what the law said about eligibility, social workers who visited welfare recipients' apartments did not check for evidence that other people lived under the same roof as the families on public relief.

The result of all of this was more than a million New Yorkers on welfare, many of them legally ineligible for assistance. This victimized many beneficiaries who were not self-reliant but dependent on public relief. Those who truly could not care for themselves often got lost and shortchanged in a system far more crowded than it should have been. Meanwhile, taxpayers got stuck with a massive bill, rife with waste, fraud, and outright theft.

Finally, although Giuliani admitted that he knew little about education and the school system, he listened carefully as I discussed the failures of the Board of Education and the City University of New York to enforce high standards and spoke of the need to improve both systems. He said many times afterward that he never had heard of the term "social promotion" until I mentioned it, but that he was outraged to learn that it existed.

Giuliani and I shared the belief that students were ill-served by a massive Board of Education bureaucracy that focused more on feathering its own nest than on filling young minds with knowledge. Improving school safety and fostering increased discipline also were preconditions for boosting student accomplishment.

Giuliani began seeking an alliance, with me running for city comptroller. He knew that this could spell trouble for Mayor Dinkins, who had needed strong Hispanic support to defeat Giuliani by just 2 percentage points in 1989. Giuliani and I had not spoken personally about an alliance, but our deputies had held intensive discussions. He was deeply intrigued by the idea of cross-endorsements that could present a balanced ticket, because he wanted to form a multiparty, multiethnic coalition.

In 1989, two-thirds of Hispanic voters had backed Dinkins, but polls showed marked increases in Hispanic support for Giuliani. In any case, Hispanics were shaping up as perhaps the crucial voting bloc. An extensive survey of Latino New Yorkers indicated that Dinkins was vulnerable among this key constituency. Dinkins's own people acknowledged that they'd had trouble persuading Latinos that the mayor was sensitive to their needs. But if the Latino community felt betrayed by Dinkins, it wasn't sure about any of the other candidates either. Because of my credibility and past history in the Puerto Rican community, I could certainly persuade a great number of those voters.

The Democratic and Republican free-for-all over the race for mayor evolved into a furious courtship of me. I was invited to meet with the city's five Republican county leaders, who hoped to convince me to run for city comptroller on the Republican ticket with Giuliani. While I was in Cape Cod, Massachusetts, mulling over the Republicans' offer, Democrats were already calling me a turncoat and pressuring me to remain loyal.

The battleground was to be over white liberals—many of them Jewish, women, or homosexual—and Hispanic voters. I drew my support from both Hispanic and Jewish voters, which would give Rudy a wider pool of contributors and a much higher profile. "If we can establish a foothold with that small percentage of loyal Democrats," Rudy said, "it will make a difference in November."

What Rudy wanted to do, above all, was establish that the city of New York was governable. In the Dinkins era and even before that, the attitude was that the city could *not* be governed. City Hall pointed to studies that said, for example, that if you had a large number of police in a certain area, the crime rate was so much; when you had a small number of police, the crime rate was the same; when you had no police, the crime rate was the same. So the attitude was "Well, this is the way it is, and we can't change it. The best you can do is get a mayor who at least doesn't get into trouble." I never agreed with that. I thought we could and should make changes; there was no reason to have a city in constant crisis. When I met Rudy, we agreed that this old philosophy had to go. We talked about a platform and agreed on all items.

The first part of the platform Rudolph Giuliani and I agreed upon was to reduce crime. If you don't have people feeling secure, you can't have a city. From head and gut, from what I heard, saw, and felt, I believed that many New Yorkers, possibly enough to swing the election, would be voting on the crime issue when it got down to the choice between Dinkins and Rudolph Giuliani. It was now a personal-survival issue in New York, far more than ever before. Why not, when children were shot down outside schools and no sensible adult would walk along a dark street—or even a lighted one—without moving real fast?

The second issue was bringing back jobs to the city. Because under Dinkins, in four years, we had lost 380,000.

The third plank of the platform was education.

Fourth, the budget was far out of balance, probably by close to a billion dollars. That meant that when Rudy took over, he would have to make drastic cuts—exactly the situation the city faced when Ed Koch became mayor and I was his deputy. It was tragic that each mayor had to inherit such a disaster. We had a structural imbalance, with which no one had really tried to come to grips. I knew that the New York economy could no longer support the size and complexity of the government it was saddled with. I wanted to bring government back to the services most needed.

Fifth, eliminate city agencies that duplicated state functions. For example, we had a city Commission on Human Rights and a state Division of Human Rights. We had a city Consumer Affairs Department and a state Consumer Protection Board. These city agencies really didn't perform any significant functions that the state agencies didn't perform. And they cost taxpayers millions of dollars.

Sixth, New York must privatize (e.g., municipal hospitals). City-run hospitals should be converted into nonprofit hospitals, like New York–Presbyterian. We knew we could save hundreds of millions of dollars in the operation of the hospitals and even more by closing down the bureaucracy at 40 Worth Street.

Finally, cut taxes. If you added up these preceding approaches, you could cut billions of dollars. We could then send a signal to the business community that taxes were not going to continue to go up. We could eliminate the commercial rent tax. We could eliminate the unincorporated business tax, and we could eliminate the hotel tax. We could no longer be the city-state we used to be. We didn't have the revenues; we didn't have a million manufacturing jobs. We didn't have the Fortune 500s. We used to talk about abandoned buildings in the South Bronx. Now we talked about abandoned buildings on Wall Street. We knew we would have to come back to the most basic functions of city government: education, police, fire, sanitation, parks, libraries.

After several meetings I concluded that Giuliani and I agreed that Gotham was governable. Alas, it was not being governed by Dinkins. We agreed that since I was a Democrat and Giuliani was a Republican, we would form what we called a fusion ticket under which Giuliani would run for mayor, I would run for comptroller, and Democrat Susan Alter would run for public advocate on the Republican and Liberal Party lines.

My defection to the Giuliani camp was a blow that other Democrats, from Governor Mario Cuomo down, sought to avoid. Various blandishments were offered, including an unspecified ambassadorship and a job with the Federal Resolution Trust Corporation—inducements that amounted to "positions out of town." My law partners worried that the city's Democratic establishment would punish our firm by withholding legal business. Dinkins's campaign manager quipped, "This is not a fusion ticket. It is a *con*fusion ticket."

Clutching a microphone atop a flatbed truck at East 116th Street and Lexington Avenue in East Harlem, I announced I was joining Giuliani, the Republican, "to rebuild our great city, restoring it to a place where standards are applied and met." We picked our spot deliberately: the landmark corner that La Guardia had made famous sixty years before in his own "fusion" campaign against Tammany Hall, in a neighborhood that was now as predominantly Hispanic as it was then Italian and Jewish.

Some Hispanics jeered me for going versus the Dems. On the stump I was not spared sneers, scoldings, or blank stares. At some campaign stops, I endured snubs and chidings for jeopardizing a Democratic mayor's bid for reelection, for trying to divide minorities, for putting myself first. "I don't like what you're doing," a woman in her late twenties said as she refused to shake my hand. Many Democrats naturally resented the alliance and berated me at campaign stops for being a turncoat.

The reaction to my joining the Giuliani ticket was surprise and outrage from my Democratic colleagues, but not total shock: I had made it clear over the years that I disagreed with my fellow Democrats on many issues. I also publicly criticized the City University, the Board of Education, and Mayor Dinkins's performance on schools and other matters.

I understood that I was burning my bridges within the Democratic Party, but I believed that it had embraced a philosophy of inaction and defeatism, as if the urban crisis were insoluble and simply had to be tolerated. No one advocated change. The reform movement, in which I had played a significant part, had dissolved. The county leaders were in firm control of the party organization. The city of New York desperately needed a new direction.

While this was my most definitive break with the Democratic Party, we had been drifting apart for some time.

I was a vocal critic of the Democratic status quo on education policy. I spent years attacking social promotion, open admissions, ever-slipping educational standards, and a relaxed, "the kids are all right" attitude toward classroom discipline. These had become shibboleths among most Democrats, yet I fired on them constantly.

Also, I had fought for years against the Democratic leadership in much of Harlem. David Dinkins, Basil Paterson, Charles Rangel, and Percy Sutton ran the Harlem Democratic machine for the strict benefit of their friends, relatives, and cronies. I was not part of their inner circle. This mattered little, really, since we saw eye to eye on less and less.

Running on a fusion ticket with a Reaganite Republican prosecutor was, for me, the equivalent of filing for divorce from the Democratic Party. And it required a lot of backbreakingly vigorous campaigning.

In response to our efforts, Dinkins pulled a brace of eleventh-hour rabbits out of his hat. First he announced that the city would extend health benefits to the domestic partners of its unmarried employees, including homosexuals—an issue of great concern to gay voters whose support he wanted and something he had pledged in the past. Then the mayor was joined in the South Bronx by Henry G. Cisneros, the secretary of housing and urban development, who brought the biggest concrete gift that the Clinton administration had managed to muster for Dinkins: a $100 million grant over five years that would let the Housing Authority hire 400 additional police officers to expand its force to 2,906 officers. Neither Rudy nor I opposed the domestic-partnership policy. But we asked the mayor to first tell us the deficit and then tell us how he was going to fund it.

When the votes were counted, I lost the comptroller's race,

but Giuliani beat Dinkins by a margin of less than 2 percent—a precise reversal of fortune from four years earlier. The Hispanic votes that I attracted to our ticket clearly contributed to his victory.

Following the election Giuliani appointed me to a committee to select a new police commissioner. The mayor-elect knew I felt as strongly as he did about the need to reduce crime. After we'd interviewed many candidates, I supported and voted for William Bratton. He had been Boston's police commissioner and earlier had cut crime as New York City's transit police chief. Bratton had a firm conviction that crime could be controlled.

Once he was appointed, Bratton built a first-rate team that included the late and legendary Jack Maple. This dapper gentleman, who wore spats to work, developed the idea of COMPSTAT, under which police used crime statistics and precinct maps to pinpoint crime day by day and move speedily to deploy police assets in the places where criminals plied their trade. As arrests climbed, crime plunged. This, and other innovations, dramatically decreased lawlessness. These crime reductions continue to the present day. Indeed, these "community policing" techniques have been copied successfully by every major city in the nation. Today New York City is America's safest metropolis. Every type of crime has dropped and stayed down in the Big Apple. The number of murders, which peaked at 2,245 in 1990 under Dinkins, had fallen to just 540 in 2005—a staggering

75.9 percent decline. Obviously many of the lives saved were those of Hispanics. So while relations with Giuliani and Bratton in the Hispanic community were not perfect, we held town meetings in Hispanic areas that indicated to us that people approved of Giuliani's anticrime policies. Indeed, the proof that high crime rates need not be tolerated but in fact can be reversed is a permanent part of Giuliani's legacy. Likewise, the foolish search for crime's "root causes" is dead and buried. Giuliani answered that question once and for all: The root cause of crime is criminals.

Giuliani triumphed spectacularly in several other areas. One of them was reducing the welfare rolls, even before President Clinton signed federal welfare reform into law. There were 1,112,490 New Yorkers on welfare in 1993. Giuliani reduced that figure 58.4 percent, to 462,595. He required able-bodied welfare recipients to apply for work. He also instructed those on welfare to identify themselves to city personnel. Thousands of those engaged in welfare fraud never showed up and were purged from the rolls.

Giuliani's 1993 election was a milestone in the reconsideration of urban liberalism in cities across the country. Like Richard Riordan in Los Angeles, Giuliani had assembled a new urban coalition composed of whites unhappy over crime and taxes, and Latinos, Asians, and other recent immigrants uncertain that their interests were served by the historic civil-rights model of minority politics. Giuliani's victory in New York signaled a dramatic opening of the cities to new directions on issues such as crime, welfare, and the reform of the great gray municipal bureaucracies.

It was an uphill battle. When, after his election, Giuliani passed a small jewelry stand just below 126th Street, the owner, a thin, wiry black man with a goatee, called out, "If you mess up, we will tear this city apart."

Rudy got a stormy reception when a Bronx town-hall meeting repeatedly erupted into boos and jeers. Police Commissioner Bratton, Deputy Mayor Ninfa Segarra, and I were also resoundingly booed by the crowd of about a thousand mainly black and Hispanic residents of the East Bronx who had packed into the auditorium of Adlai Stevenson High School. The mayor remained poised despite frequent interruptions and calmly pleaded for respect. "Now, that isn't fair," Rudy said in response to a chant of "Where's the jobs?" "I don't shout in the middle of your questions. You shouldn't shout when I'm trying to answer your questions."

Under Rudy, crime was reduced. The crime rate went way down, and the city was far more secure. There were still all kinds of problems, but the reality was, we had to give credit to Rudy for the fact that we'd had two thousand murders a year under Dinkins, and under Rudy we had less than a quarter of that number. Some innocent people did get killed because the police made errors. That happened under Dinkins, too. But due to the new policies, we had hundreds and hundreds of people—thousands of them—who were *not* being killed. The most dramatic example of the difference was pointed up in a *New York Times* column by Stanley Crouch, who noted that in 1990, 1,096 black people were murdered and in 1999, 356 were murdered. So when people say that poor black people were killed by Giuliani's police, they should look at all the people Giuliani's police had saved from getting killed. The same thing with Hispanics and other groups.

When the convention centers had blackballed New York City because they didn't want to pay the hotel tax, Rudy reduced it. New York City became available for conventions, and the additional conventions filled up hotel rooms; new hotels were built to meet the new demand. At the same time, ironically, the reduced hotel tax brought in more revenue than it had before, by increasing the volume of business. So the supply-side argument, despite its critics, is not totally stupid.

Jobs returned to the city, because of the reduction in crime and because of many other policies that Rudy implemented. Far more came back than the 380,000 we had lost under Dinkins.

Rudy got the Mafia out of the Fulton Fish Market. More important, we moved to get the mob out of the garbage-collection business. Rudy went after them, and as a result a lot of people were indicted and driven out of the garbage-collection business.

The cost of commercial garbage collection went down by about 40 percent: Garbage collection had been subject to a "tax," in the form of high, Mafia-controlled rates and demands for bribes. Rudy put an end to this, helping in yet one more way to bring new business to New York.

Racial profiling was not the evil it was made out to be. In the neighborhoods where people were stopped and searched, blacks were identified as perpetrators of 63 percent of violent crimes, Hispanics were identified as perpetrators of 26 percent of violent crimes, whites 8 percent, and 2.3 percent for others. Of those who were stopped, 52 percent were black, 32 percent Hispanic, and 13 percent white. So you have 63 percent of violent crimes being perpetrated by blacks and 52 percent of those being stopped are black—not an unreasonable figure. Similarly, when you have 26 percent of the crimes committed by Hispanics and 32 percent of those being stopped are Hispanic, that is also comparable. The ratio of blacks and Hispanics among those being stopped and frisked was not out of line with the ratio of blacks and Hispanics committing crimes.

Working closely with Giuliani showed me what I believed all along: Competent leadership, vision, and accountability could all lead to a renaissance on the Hudson. Decades of liberal misrule under multiple Democrats and the left-wing Republican-turned-Democrat John Lindsay had brought the city to its knees. Within a few months of Giuliani's inauguration, however, crime and disorder were declining while personal security and a city-wide sense of optimism were on the way up. City officials who lounged at work suddenly realized that they had better do their jobs—or else. New Yorkers began to expect value for their high (yet falling) taxes, and City Hall delivered.

After this campaign I very publicly switched my registration to Republican. Standing beneath two sparkling chandeliers at the headquarters of the Women's National Republican Club, flanked by Mayor Giuliani and members of the Republican National Committee, I signed a GOP voter-registration card. As a lifelong Democrat, I did not make this decision lightly. But in the end I had no choice. The New York State Democratic Party has remained in the past and cannot make things better, because its members don't understand what is wrong. Over the years, I found myself disagreeing more and more with city and state Democratic policies and positions. For decades, Democratic leaders had advocated the same old solutions with no accountability and came up with the same old failures. In contrast, the Republican Party demonstrated a willingness to realistically address the vital issues we faced. Hard experience convinced me that Democratic leaders are never going to change.

I felt increasingly that the Democratic Party took large portions of its constituency for granted. Too many die-hard Dems, locally as well as nationally, continued to cling to the tired slogans of generations past as if they were a political life raft. Workfare was anathema to Democrats, but not to me. As Assemblyman Roberto Ramirez put it, "The fact is that Badillo has been espousing Republican ideology for quite a few years now. . . . Most of us wondered what took him so long."

Giuliani's mayoralty radically transformed not only my political orientation but New York City as a whole. As he left office in 2002, no one was calling Gotham "the ungovernable city." David Dinkins had talked the talk about a "gorgeous mosaic," but his lenient liberal policies had only deepened divisions of race and class. By asking more of all New Yorkers, Giuliani brought the once-fractious city together, as the intercultural displays of solidarity after 9/11 cast into bold relief. In the next chapter, therefore, I will consider how some of the same ideas that unified New York City can unify America as a whole.

9

Toward a Unified Culture

ALMOST FROM THE day I arrived in New York, as I have said, it was clear to me that in the United States you are judged by the color of your skin. At the same time, it is obvious from walking around midtown Manhattan that no metropolis in the world can boast so many individuals from all races and all nations who live and work in such close proximity to one another. The city houses citizens from some 200 nations who speak 173 languages, according to the May 2005 issue of *Wired* magazine. This is why New York is nicknamed "the Capital of the World." For a two-dollar fare, you can experience a virtual United Nations in any subway car at rush hour.

As a long-distance runner, I have completed eleven New York City marathons. Marathon Day every November is the one occasion when millions of New Yorkers come outdoors to cheer us on for all 26.2 miles of each race. We pass through every borough, starting in Staten Island (populated predominantly by Italians), run through Brooklyn (with its Irish, Hasidic Jewish, African-American, Polish, Caribbean, and Hispanic neighborhoods), pass into Queens (German, Greek, Irish, Italian, Asian), then Manhattan (Jews, WASPs, Hispanics), then the Bronx (blacks and Hispanics), and back into Manhattan (Harlem's blacks), ending at Central Park's Tavern on the Green. Every conceivable nationality joins in the celebration. The most exciting experience for us runners, aside from finishing the race, is the knowledge that for all of the city's problems, the people of New York respond as one. This sense of unity was apparent as well on the morning of September 11, 2001, when America was attacked. There was neither panic nor looting, just a grim resolve to deal with a tragic loss of lives.

Why, then, can't we present ourselves as a unified culture? Why do we divide ourselves into majority and minority groups? Why do we refer to one group of our people as white and another as "people of color"? Because when we set up such divisions, we really are saying, even if subconsciously, that one group is superior to the other. We further intensify such divisions when we establish racial-preference programs to grant special privileges to allegedly disadvantaged groups. Whatever benefits such programs provide are lost because of the stigma that adheres to the beneficiaries. Most important, what purpose do we achieve from dividing ourselves by race? I experienced one of the most tragic results of this division while still in school—the incident with my friend Keith mentioned earlier.

Nevertheless, I have often thought about this moment, because it showed me that America's rigid racism—which I acknowledge is not politically correct to discuss but which is still evident to those who come from a different culture—damages individuals and made me determined to avoid the pitfalls of racial polarization, not just for myself but for the Puerto Rican and larger Hispanic community to which I belong. I have come to believe that the most important contribution Latin Americans can make to America is to avoid racial labels, to refuse to divide themselves along color lines, and to stay united as a group so we may show the larger society that it is possible to relate to each other without being separated by the wall of racism. I have always resisted the idea that the Hispanic community should split itself internally along racial lines. Indeed, that's how the term "Hispanic" originated. When I first got into politics, the Census Bureau forms required that individuals identify themselves as "White," "Black," or "Asian." Together with others I argued before the census officials that in Hispanic communities there are people who are white, black, Asian, and a mixture of every conceivable race. I pointed out that if Hispanics categorized themselves by race, they would fall into the same trap that has poisoned U.S. race relations. Among others, I proposed a new category, "Hispanic," which would cover our entire community. The Census Bureau agreed, and census forms since the year 1980 have included this particular category.

I listed myself, and never thought twice about doing so, as "Hispanic" in every census. Many Hispanics, though not all, do the same. Naturally, this further confuses efforts to describe America's population by race. This is a good thing, I think, because I do not believe in racial categories and consider them harmful and literally divisive. Latin Americans do not racially pigeonhole themselves and thus get along much better as a society.

This does not mean that Hispanics are not aware that some people are white, some black, some Asian, some from particular countries such as Ireland, Italy, Germany, Poland, or Russia. Of course they know these facts, and naturally people are going to be proud of their native countries. But this should not be a basis for setting official governmental policy. Such laws develop from simply counting kids in a classroom by color to assuming that those of one skin tone are disadvantaged while others are advantaged. Soon people start to think that somehow their skin color is undesirable.

None of this means that we should not help those in need. There are many poor people in America, and there are many people who suffer severe disadvantages. A better way to address these problems is to define them by economic class rather than by race. Thus a program to help the poor move into the middle class, for instance, would apply to all low-income people, regardless of race. This is how it should be.

All existing government programs could be redesigned to eliminate racial stigma. For example, in the 1960s Americans knew they had to find a way to help students from poor families with educational disadvantages gain admission to the City University of New York. At that time CUNY's admissions standards were very high, and very few black or Hispanic students could meet them because they had graduated from high schools with dismal educational standards.

The plan I developed, along with others, was SEEK, a prebaccalaureate program at City College of New York, enacted by the New York state legislature in 1966 as CUNY's higher-education opportunity program. Its purpose was to provide access to CUNY for poor students who'd graduated from high schools that had not prepared them for the rigors of college. The criteria for admission to SEEK require that a student:

- have a gross family income at or below New York State's definition of poverty
- be a high-school graduate or recipient of a state-approved equivalency diploma

- be inadmissible according to the freshman admissions criteria for CUNY senior colleges
- demonstrate, through a basic skills test, the potential for success in college

Notice the absence of race as a criterion. In essence a student has to show only that he or she is poor and has graduated from an inferior high school. Once admitted to college, the SEEK student gets an array of instructional, financial, and counseling support services. Program activities are designed to assist students in meeting the challenges of college and to provide a supportive environment in which they will flourish.

In their nearly forty years of existence, the SEEK and College Discovery program, which is SEEK's equivalent for two-year community colleges, together have enrolled approximately 230,000 low-income students of all races. Without university access to these programs, most would not have been able to earn the college degrees that afforded them entry into the professions and the middle class. Program students have gone on to win the Gates Millennium Scholarship, the Woodrow Wilson Fellowship, the Mellon Minority Fellowship, and other local, state, and national awards.

In the 2004–2005 school year, there were more than 12,000 students at CUNY enrolled in SEEK and College Discovery. Approximately 13 percent were white, 18 percent Asian, 23 percent black, and 40 percent Hispanic. This is the type of program that would be regarded as a racial-preference program if it excluded whites, but because it is open to all races, it has avoided the criticisms that engulf racial-preference programs. At the same time, its benefits are clearly impressive.

With a little ingenuity, America could redesign today's government programs so that they could reach all who need them without scarring them with racist labels. We then would be well on the way to eliminating such categories as "African-American," "Asian-American," and "Hispanic-American"—the one I myself helped to institute on the census—and simply call ourselves Americans who share a unified culture.

Of course, those in the Hispanic community have to do their part to move this country toward a unified culture. This means that they must strive to become full-fledged members of the larger society without requiring that it make special allowances for them. They should emphasize that they do not seek any special benefits and that they are confident of their ability to compete with any group. They should explain that they have as much talent as anyone else and can go toe-to-toe in any economic endeavor, just as their athletes, who are so outstanding on the baseball diamond, do not ask for anything other than to demonstrate their ability. Hispanics have shown throughout the countries of Latin America that they have among them talented doctors, lawyers, professors, philosophers, novelists, artists, engineers, businessmen, and people who have been successful in every area. They do not become any less able as a group when they migrate to the United States. To those who would seek to discriminate against them and argue that they are not competent to participate fully in this society, their answer should be that they have already proved their ability to participate in a complex society in the countries from which they emigrated.

There is no question that the Hispanics who have come here illegally in the past twenty to twenty-five years are predominantly poor, uneducated people who work in unskilled jobs. The New Hispanic Center reported in 2006 that illegal immigrants hold 17 percent of all jobs in cleaning and building maintenance, 14 percent of all construction jobs, and 12 percent of food-preparation jobs. Female illegal immigrants hold a substantial percentage of household jobs.

Analyzing these figures, Linda Chavez notes:

The Census Bureau confirms that a great many immigrants are imbued with an entrepreneurial spirit that puts to shame those of us who were born here. It reports that Hispanics are opening up businesses three times faster than the national average. There were almost 1.6 million Hispanic-owned businesses generating $222 billion in revenue in 2002, the year for which the census collected data. And nearly one quarter of these opened between 1997 and 2002. . . .

Most of these businesses are family affairs, with few employees. But more than 1,500 nationwide employed 100 or more people, generating $42 billion in gross receipts.

Nearly 30 percent of Hispanic-owned businesses were in construction, repair, maintenance or other personal services, while 36 percent were in retail or wholesale trade. The largest numbers were concentrated in California and Texas, home to the biggest Mexican-American and Mexican immigrant populations. . . .

Hispanic entrepreneurs are becoming an increasingly vital part of the economic engine that drives this nation. Hispanics aren't turning the U.S. into a Latin American outpost; they are being transformed into the quintessential American: the small and not-so-small businessman and woman.[1]

In an article in the *New York Post* of March 27, 2006, Sandra Guzman offers an example of how well New York City's Hispanic entrepreneurs are doing:

Word that Hispanics are opening businesses faster than any other ethnic group in the nation hardly comes as a surprise to NYU grad Ariel Aparicio.

The Cuban-born entrepreneur owns two thriving Thai restaurants in Brooklyn and is self-financing a music career.

"We are hardworking people," he said. "And came to this country to make a better life for ourselves and our families."

The Census Department seems to agree, reporting last week that Hispanics owned nearly 1.6 million businesses in 2002—a 31 percent jump from just five years earlier.

During the same period, the number of Hispanic businesses zoomed by nearly 60 percent in New York—the biggest growth rate of any state.

Aparicio and Andrew Jerro opened the Cobble Hill restaurant Joya over six years ago. Last spring, Song opened in Park Slope. Together, they employed about 25 people and raked in over a half-million dollars a year.

"From the date we opened, we were a hit," Aparicio said. "We were profitable our first year. . . .

"We borrowed from family and friends and took out small-business loans to come up with the $250,000 to open Joya," Aparicio recalled.

He started Bully Records five years ago and has recorded three punk-rock albums. His latest, "Frolic and F***," is set to hit stores this month.

Not that he fears his restaurants will suffer as his music career takes off.

"With good time management," he said, "anything is possible."

Columnist David Brooks also weighed in with a heartfelt pro-immigrant piece:

My first argument is that the exclusionists are wrong when they say the current wave of immigration is tearing our social fabric. The facts show that the recent rise in immigration hasn't been accompanied by social breakdown, but by social repair. As immigration has surged, violent crime has fallen by 57 percent. Teen pregnancies and abortion rates have declined by a third. Teenagers are having fewer sexual partners and losing their virginity later. Teen suicide rates have dropped. The divorce rate for young people is on the way down. . . .

My second argument is that the immigrants themselves are like a booster shot of traditional morality injected into the body politic. Immigrants work hard. They build community groups. They have traditional ideas about family structure, and they work heroically to make them a reality. . . .

My third argument is that good values lead to success, and that immigrants' long-term contributions more than compensate for the short-term strains they cause. There's no use denying the strains immigration imposes on schools, hospitals and wage levels in some markets (but economists are sharply divided on this).

So over the long haul, today's immigrants succeed. By the second generation, most immigrant families are middle class and paying taxes that more than make up for the costs of the first generation. By the third generation, 90 percent speak English fluently and 50 percent marry non-Latinos. . . .

Please ask yourself this: As we contemplate America's moral fiber, do the real threats come from immigrants, or are some people merely blaming them for sins that are already here?[2]

During demonstrations in New York City in support of immigrants' rights, the sentiments toward this country were expressed as follows, according to a report in the April 2, 2006, *New York Times:*

"We came here because we love America and we want to stay here," said Liliana Melgarejo, 31, who immigrated from Argentina 13 years ago and works in Manhattan as a housekeeper. . . . "My children are American. I love my country, too, but there is no future there. Here, they can be a doctor, anything."

Ms. Melgarejo, who carried an American flag, also weighed in on the presence of the foreign flags at yesterday's march and at others across the country, something that critics have seized upon as a symbol of recent immigrants' unwillingness to fully embrace their adopted country.

"That is not the message we want to send," she said. "I feel that they should take the biggest American flag they can find and wave it in the air."

There is no doubt in my mind that Hispanics will be absorbed into American life, just as the Italians, Germans, Jews, and Irish have been. That does not mean that they have to abandon their individual culture. All the other groups have maintained their culture while becoming a part of the larger community, and they, as Hispanics, will do the same.

During my first term in Congress, I represented a Greek population in Astoria, Queens. I went to many functions in the Greek community and found that they had maintained their religion, their culture, and all their traditions while participating fully in the life of New York City. The only time they called attention to themselves was during the annual Greek Independence

Day Parade along Fifth Avenue, where thousands marched on a Sunday in the spring.

A unified culture, therefore, is possible without a loss of identity. The pattern has been set in this country, and Hispanics will be one more group to join this remarkable odyssey.

10

The Hispanic Community in the United States and Latin America: The Next Fifty Years

Hispanics are now, as I have observed, America's largest minority. At 42 million in 2006, we constitute 14.2 percent of the total U.S. population, not including Puerto Rico's 4 million residents. In the next fifty years, our numbers are projected to grow to over 120 million—equal to 24 percent of America's population—thanks to natural birth rates and continued immigration, both legal and illegal. Accordingly, we can expect our influence to grow in every aspect of American life.

Most dramatically, there is an imminent explosion in the number of eligible voters that could prove decisive in national politics and in the largest states of the union. I have already mentioned that in 2004 there were thirteen states where people of Hispanic origin constitute more than 10 percent of the population. Although the number of registered voters is low (e.g., 6 percent in the 2004 elections), there is no doubt that the Hispanic vote could be decisive in the 2008 presidential elections. This explains the controversy surrounding the immigration-reform legislation in 2006. The Republicans in the House of Representatives, most of whose districts constitute just portions of particular states, passed legislation to provide strict border security, including building a wall on the southern border, and for punishment of illegal immigrants and anyone who assists them. Senate Republicans, who represent entire states, did not want to antagonize Hispanic voters and sought to approve compromise legislation that would enable many illegal immigrants to work their way toward citizenship. Democrats in both chambers were anxious to retain the Hispanic vote and resisted the GOP-led punitive measures. President Bush much earlier had proposed a guest-worker program and used his limited influence to advance compromise legislation between the House's hard-liner package and the Senate's softer measure.

The underlying factor that governs this debate is the reality that the Hispanic vote has been moving steadily toward the Republican Party. At a March 2004 meeting at Long Island's Republic Airport, I told President Bush in Spanish that he should do his television commercials in Spanish and speak more in Spanish to Hispanic groups. If he did so, I predicted, his share of the Hispanic vote would climb from 34 percent in 2000 to 45 percent in 2004.

The president told me, in Spanish, that he did not think he spoke Spanish that well. I told him that he obviously did—we had, after all, been speaking in Spanish throughout our entire conversation. He seemed to realize I was right, and he instructed his aides to remind him of this when he returned to Washington. He told me afterward that he followed my advice, and on Election Day he received 44 percent of the Hispanic vote. This proves that the Democratic Party no longer can take the Hispanic vote for granted. Meanwhile, President Bush got only 11 percent of the African-American vote, which shows that the black community still is very much attached to the Democratic Party.

Both parties know that the entire Hispanic community will rise in protest when there is an attempt to demonize immigrants or Hispanics. That happened when Governor Pete Wilson (R-California) backed a 1994 initiative to exclude illegal immigrants from public schools and services. The initiative passed. After twelve years many analysts believe that the Hispanic backlash in the wake of this initiative wrecked the California Republican Party for a decade.[1]

Traditionally Hispanics have supported Democratic presidents, such as Franklin Roosevelt, John Kennedy, and Lyndon

Johnson, because the Democratic Party used government's power to help the poor and minorities. (The Cuban community remains anomalously Republican, as if they blame President Kennedy for the 1961 Bay of Pigs disaster that enabled Castro to remain in power.)

Yet the culture and traditions of the Hispanic community are conservative when it comes to social issues such as abortion, gay rights, women's rights, or federal and state aid to parochial schools. These conservative leanings are reinforced not only by the predominant influence of Catholicism but also by the rising Hispanic ratio in Pentecostal Protestant sects, which are arguably even more conservative. This social conservatism is shifting the Hispanic community toward the Republican Party, much as it moved blue-collar Caucasian workers to the GOP in the 1970s and 1980s. This could mean large Republican majorities as the rapidly growing Hispanic community enters the middle class.

In the meantime most Hispanics remain in poverty, or barely above it, with low educational achievement, language problems, inadequate health insurance, housing shortages, and mostly dismal employment opportunities. Some enterprising Hispanic businessmen have begun to establish themselves in areas such as supermarkets, construction, and franchises, but many have had difficulty raising capital to expand.

The United States is a postindustrial economy. Today we live in an information society. Now more than ever, the key to advancement is educational achievement.

Too many Hispanics remain dependent on government for jobs, housing, health care, and other necessities.

As a former congressman and deputy mayor, and as a public servant who moreover *supported* programs in those areas, I can assure everyone that government is not geared to meet those needs. The only answer to the problem of Hispanic poverty and assimilation, as I have stressed time and again, is education. If Hispanic children enjoy great schooling, earning college degrees and postgraduate diplomas when their chosen professions require them, they will secure their own jobs, provide their own housing, finance their own health care, and meet their own families' economic needs. Many other immigrant groups have used educational success as the staircase to climb out of poverty and into the middle and upper classes. We must climb the same staircase today.

Any long climb takes effort, and serious educational achievement requires serious effort—not just by individual students but by entire families and the whole Hispanic community. Hispanics must set aside talk of their great culture, their music, and their traditions and instead focus on educational accomplishment.

America's educational standards and policies are largely detrimental to Hispanics. These policies persist because few speak out against them and insist forcefully enough that they be changed. Hispanic parents rarely get involved with their children's schools. They seldom attend parent-teacher conferences, ensure that children do their homework, or inspire their children to dream of attending college. Many Hispanic parents seem to accept the characterization of their community as a minority group, something they would find incomprehensible in the Latin and Caribbean countries from which they come. They accept labels such as "brown people" or "people of color." Having gone along with such characterizations, some Hispanics behave as if they actually were a persecuted ethnic group, with a permanently diminished capacity for success.

They find excuses to justify their nonperformance. They say they live in poverty and cannot be expected to accomplish what middle-class or "white" people do. They cite language problems as impediments to progress. They say, above all, that they are victims of discrimination and thus cannot move ahead.

None of these arguments is valid. Other groups, including many nonwhite groups, faced the same problems when they arrived and have overcome them. The future of American Hispanics is bound up with a problem that nobody seems to want to confront. Illegal immigration could mean dozens of millions more Hispanics entering this country in the next fifty years. Some legislators, and many ordinary citizens, assume that our borders can be secured either by hiring more Border Patrol officers to prevent unlawful crossings or by punishing employers who hire illegal immigrants. None of this will happen. The people who are coming here from Mexico, Central and South America, and the Dominican Republic are escaping economic disasters. Their migration stems from their inescapable knowledge that they will not be able to feed themselves or their families in their native lands and that there is no economic program whatsoever in place to improve their standard of living. They are fleeing economic deprivation. In the history of the world, no migration based on economic necessity has ever been halted with police measures.

The only way to stop the current wave of economic migration is by taking steps to improve the economies of the countries from which the immigrants are coming. It is clear from the history of these countries, the five-century siesta I discussed earlier, that their economic conditions will not improve by themselves in the near future. A way must be found to develop successful aid programs from outside.

The first step, however, is for Latin countries to recognize their urgent responsibility to improve their own economic conditions. I have detected among Latin policy makers a reluctance, indeed an outright refusal, to recognize that these structural problems exist. When I was in Congress, I met with the Mexican president and members of Mexico's congress and made many attempts to discuss the issue. But they refused to engage in any conversation on the subject, even though they knew that I supported amnesty for immigrants and sympathized with their cause. Mexico's outgoing president, as of this writing, Vicente Fox, in a work he published prior to being elected to office, acknowledged "that so many Mexicans are living in the United States because our bad Federal government did not allow them to get ahead here in their own country."[2]

Yet Fox did not develop any meaningful strategy to improve conditions in Mexico. Instead illegal immigration from Mexico has increased on his watch.

I read the Spanish newspapers every day. Never once have I read any indication from the leaders of any Latin American country that they consider themselves at all responsible for the migrations of their populations to the United States, except to recognize that the amounts of money these immigrants send home has become a significant contribution to their economies. It is no surprise that these leaders do not want to recognize that their failure to improve their economies impels the migration of their citizens to the United States. Such admissions would highlight their shortcomings and perhaps force them to bring about the kind of fundamental institutional reforms that they consistently refuse to undertake.

For example, they need to create a system of laws that cannot be changed at the whim of whoever happens to be elected chief executive. This includes a permanent written constitution, a legislative body that cannot be abolished by the executive, and a truly independent judiciary. In addition, these leaders need to take steps to eliminate the systemic corruption that plagues so many Latin American states. Eduardo Buscaglia, of the Hoover Institution, argues that

the probability of detecting corruption decreases as corruption becomes more systemic. Therefore, as corruption becomes more systemic, enforcement measures of the traditional kind affecting the expected punishment of committing illicit acts become less effective and other preventive measures, such as organizational changes (e.g., reducing procedural complexities in the provision of public services), salary increases, and other measures, become much more effective.[3]

Buscaglia also suggests that

civil society should become involved [in] implementing and monitoring the anticorruption policies. The action plan should be developed through consensus between civil society and government and contain problems, solutions, deadlines for implementation of solutions, and expected results.

Buscaglia points out that this approach has been applied at the judicial and municipal levels in many countries, with significant results. He also concludes that entrenched political interests often resist or delay reforms. The main point is, however, that systemic corruption does exist in many countries and that specific procedures have been devised to root it out.

Once necessary institutional reforms have been put in place and anticorruption strategies have been adopted, priorities have to be established to bring about real improvement. The Latin America expert William Ratliff delineates the reprioritization that will be required:

Mexican Nobel laureate Octavio Paz often tried to get Americans to understand the differences between themselves and Mexicans. Two decades ago he wrote, "To cross the border between [Mexico and the United States] is to change civilizations. Americans are the children of the Reformation, and their origins are those of the modern world; we Mexicans are the children of the Spanish empire, the champion of the Counterreformation, a movement that opposed the new modernity and failed." The Europeans who settled in the United States mostly fanned out from what was called "New England," while Mexico, which became the launching place for settlements in Spanish South America, was called "New

Spain." . . . A Peruvian analyst has added that "it is said that Latin America's misfortune is instability" when in fact it is just the opposite: Latin America has for centuries been marked by excessive stability.[4]

Ratliff, who has spent more than forty years living and traveling in Latin America, China, and Southeast Asia, enumerates the similarities and differences he's observed in those countries:

> Forty years ago Asia and Latin America were at about the same levels of economic and educational development. Indeed, in some cases at that time Latin America was ahead of Asia and in some respects still is. Since then, however, Latin America and reforming Asia have followed very different educational paths that were chosen by national leaders either out of conviction or expediency. . . .
>
> Whereas a major part of reforming Asia's success in joining the modern world has been its education system, a major impediment to Latin America's doing nearly as well has been its form of education. . . . The remarkable Asian growth during the last half century occurred because Asian leaders realized they had to implement major reforms, among the most important being education reforms, to grow or even survive in the modern world. And they did it.

Latin American countries, therefore, have a model to follow if they wish to improve their citizens' economic and social conditions. The United States should be willing to provide appropriate and targeted assistance. Ample use should be made of existing international agencies, such as the UN Economic Commission for Latin America and the Caribbean, the Organization of American States, and the Inter-American Development Bank.

One structure for providing this assistance could be the Caribbean Basin Initiative, originally approved by President Reagan in 1984. CBI could be expanded and strengthened to include Mexico and mainland Central and South American countries. With this, together with the Mexican Free Trade Agreement and the Central American Free Trade Agreement (CAFTA), the mechanisms for economic assistance are already available. They just need to be put to work.

A perfect example of this type of U.S.-Latin cooperation: In 1994, Pedro Rosselló González, the governor of Puerto Rico, was mounting a war on crime. He wanted CUNY's help to make his police force into a powerful and professional one. At the invitation of Gerald W. Lynch, president of CUNY's John Jay College of Criminal Justice, I visited the campus of the Puerto Rican Police Academy to study a new CUNY program in Puerto Rico to train police officers and confer on them an associate degree in police science. The CUNY trustees approved the proposal in March. Puerto Rico was almost an air bridge to

New York. We had an affinity and an interest in helping them, and we were asked to help. We saw it as very compatible with our mission of combining training and education.

This may sound modest and small-scale. But it is important to remember that even a relatively modest economic improvement might mean a huge difference in those countries whose huddled masses illegally enter America. In this respect the economic story of Puerto Rico in the twentieth century may serve as an object lesson in any attempt to stem the tide of immigration.

In the 1930s and early 1940s, Puerto Rico resembled the poorest Third World countries. After the Second World War, nearly one third of Puerto Ricans immigrated to America, mostly to New York City. When Luis Muñoz Marín was elected governor in 1948, he began a historic campaign of economic reforms under the rubric Operation Bootstrap. As these reforms, together with the newly strengthened University of Puerto Rico, helped establish a new, indigenous middle class, the emigration tapered off. The tipping point came when the per capita income of the average Puerto Rican reached one-half of the per capita income of the average resident of Mississippi, the lowest in all the fifty states. Therefore, it is not necessary to bring the per capita income of Mexico and other Latin American countries to the level of the United States. It is only essential to improve economic conditions and education opportunities to the point where a significant middle class develops. This will lead to a further expansion of the middle class, convincing people that there is a real opportunity for change. We must remember that Puerto Ricans did not want to leave Puerto Rico, and Latin Americans did not want to leave their countries. It is just that they did not have any chance of improvement at the present time.

What Latin America needs is an economic overhaul. Reform is possible; serious improvements in the lives of average citizens in Latin America can and must be achieved. If America wants to avoid the difficulties of continued illegal immigration in the next fifty years, this is the only way.

11

One Nation, One Standard

THE 2006 CONGRESSIONAL debate over immigration legislation spotlighted the huge increase in illegal Hispanic immigration to the United States in the last fifty years. Illegal immigration made headlines in every newspaper and was the subject of editorial comment for weeks. Radio talk shows and television network and cable programs featured impassioned discussions of the subject. Suddenly the security of the Mexican border became the most important issue in the minds of most Americans and legislators. President George W. Bush visited the area in Arizona where it was alleged that four thousand to six thousand illegals "sneaked" into the United States every night.

Within days after the president's speech, the United States Senate followed the House of Representatives in voting for building a wall several hundred miles long at the border between the United States and Mexico in order to curtail illegal immigration.

All this saturation coverage of illegal immigration focused the nation's attention on the Hispanic community, which accounts for over 80 percent of illegal immigration. And the more attention that was focused on the Hispanic community, the more the underlying argument became whether Hispanics in such large numbers could be assimilated into American culture as other groups had been, with the subliminal suggestion that it would not be possible because these new immigrants were too different from the previous ones. It was almost as if the burden of proof had shifted from the acceptance of immigrants as people who wanted to participate in the American Dream to a demand that the new Hispanic population prove itself worthy of remaining within our borders. The United States Senate overwhelmingly approved an amendment declaring English to be the national language. The House of Representatives passed a law providing that illegal aliens were guilty of a felony punishable by five years' imprisonment. Clearly, there are great fears about the impact the millions of Hispanics could have on the culture of the country.

Acknowledging these fears in his book *Assimilation, American Style,* Dr. Peter D. Salins reflects:

In view of current hand-wringing about the prospects of living with today's new immigrants, the most important question is this: Why was America's immigration experiment so successful in the past? That the United States was able to absorb and integrate generation upon generation of immigrants from impossibly disparate ethnic backgrounds, while holding on to—indeed strengthening—its fundamental liberties and principles, was a remarkable achievement, unreplicated in any other nation. But the experiment could, under the wrong set of circumstances, just as easily have gone awry. That it did not was due, in no small measure, to natives and immigrants agreeing to subscribe to the three unities of the assimilation contract: the cultural unity imposed by uncompromised English language dominance, the civic unity imposed by pride in being American and allegiance to the American Idea, and the unity of values imposed by adherence (in a one-third Catholic nation) to the Protestant ethic. It was especially important that immigrants and natives worked together to assimilate the immigrants' children and grandchildren.[1]

This three-pronged formula has historically formed the basis of assimilation of all previous immigrant groups who arrived in this country. English-language dominance guaranteed cultural unity, and while there were attempts to legitimatize other languages, such as German during the heavy German immigration, and though German immigrants such as Carl Schurz were passionate advocates of bilingualism, every legislative effort to approve German bilingualism was defeated. I knew this when I supported the Bilingual Education Act of 1974, and in fact I was surprised that it was approved by my colleagues given the historical aversion to any language other than English. I was even more surprised when the "Badillo amendment" to the Voting Rights Act of 1975 approved voting in Spanish. Since then, bilingualism in education and in voting has been extended to many other languages. As a result, there are many who fear that the cultural unity imposed by an English-only society is in danger of coming apart.

The second premise of assimilation, as expressed by Dr. Salins, "the civic unity imposed by pride in being American and allegiance to the American Idea," was promoted by a universal system of education that emphasized the Declaration of Independence, the inspiring story of our Founding Fathers, the permanence of the Constitution, and the pride in a society founded on the concept that "all men are created equal." This American Idea also made it easier to accept immigrants from all nations, since we would all be a part of one united society. In the last fifty years, assimilation—which Dr. Salins defines as "a comprehensive social and cultural unification of the American population, the breaking down not only of ethnic barriers among American schoolchildren, but those of class and regions as well"—has been challenged by an antiassimilationist ideology, which is called "multiculturalism" or "ethnocentricity" or "ethnic federalism," and which is specifically identified with the Hispanic community.

In his book *The Disuniting of America*, Arthur M. Schlesinger Jr., an old-line liberal, notes the destructive influence of this new-left ideology.

> Ethnic ideologues . . . have set themselves against the old American ideal of assimilation. They call on this republic to think in terms not of individual but of group identity and to move the policy from individual to group rights. They have made a certain progress in transforming the United States into a more segregated society. They have filled the air with recrimination and rancor and have remarkably advanced the fragmentation of American life.[2]

The ethnic federalism that Professor Schlesinger writes about is expressed in the recent movement toward Latino studies in universities and multicultural events on college campuses. It is also the basis for affirmative-action programs and, more recently, for the movement to establish the rights of immigrants as a new "civil-rights movement."

Fortunately, the third prong of assimilation as defined by Dr. Salins, "the unity of values imposed by adherence . . . to the Protestant ethic," is not threatened by the influx of Hispanics, because the one area of agreement among all sides is that Hispanics are willing to work and that they will accept jobs that most Americans will not accept under conditions that are in violation of labor standards. The New Hispanic Center has estimated in 2006 that 24 percent of agricultural workers, 36 percent of insulation workers, 29 percent of roofers, 28 percent of drywall installers, and 12 percent of food-preparation workers are undocumented. These jobs and housekeeping work are generally the most undesirable employment, but at the same time they are essential to a well-ordered society.

The debate between those who support the established formula for assimilation and those who argue that multiculturalism should prevail has been going on in intellectual circles for more than twenty-five years. Those who demand special rights for Hispanics are the Mexican American Legal Defense and Education Fund, the Puerto Rican Legal Defense and Education Fund, the National Council of La Raza, Aspira, and other Hispanic organizations. Those who oppose them and continue to promote assimilation include Linda Chavez, Arthur Schlesinger Jr., Harvard professor Stephan Thernstrom and his wife and co-author, Abigail, and the Manhattan Institute (a New York think tank).

In *Out of the Barrio: Toward a New Politics of Hispanic Assimilation,* Chavez wrote:

> Now ethnic leaders demand that their groups remain separate, that their native culture and language be preserved intact, and that whatever accommodation takes place be on the part of the receiving society. Hispanic leaders have been among the most demanding, insisting that Hispanic children be taught in Spanish; that Hispanic adults be allowed to cast their ballots in their native language and that they have the right to vote in districts in which Hispanics make up the majority of voters; that their ethnicity entitles them to a certain percentage of jobs and college admissions; that immigrants from Latin America be granted many of these same benefits, even if they are in the country illegally.

What is different now is that as a result of the national debate on illegal immigration and the competing legislative proposals in the House of Representatives and the Senate, the opposing points of view that were once limited to debates among intellectuals are now part of a genuine national conversation. There is hardly anyone in the nation who is not aware that we have somewhere between 11 and 20 million illegal aliens in the country, mostly Hispanics. We all know now that the borders of this country are not secure, and we have all seen television footage of Mexicans and other Hispanics crossing illegally into this country. We are all certain that more Hispanics are preparing to leave their countries and come to the United States. Some of us have even heard the frightening poll taken by the Pew Hispanic Center stating that 49 percent of all Mexican adults would come to the United States if they could. We have also seen the televised report that 25 percent of illegals are visa overstays, which indicates that building walls at the border would not be a definitive solution to illegal immigration.

What has taken place is that the American public has been presented with the specter of a massive invasion of illegal Hispanic immigrants who are already within our borders and who intend to come in even larger numbers in the immediate future. These immigrants are seen to be demanding legalization or even amnesty and are not seen to be eager to learn English or to accept our values or traditions. This perception could be of incalculable damage to the Hispanic community unless more Hispanic leaders repudiate it.

We are and have been one nation, with one standard, which has been that regardless of what part of the world we may have originated from, we come here to strengthen and reinforce the culture and traditions of this country. Above all, we must be prepared to learn the English language as fast as possible so that we can be full participants in this society. We have to consider citizenship to be a privilege that requires allegiance to the American flag and our institutions. We have to be prepared to register and vote and to run for office on the basis of our abilities and not our ethnic backgrounds.

This does not mean that we have to forget our heritage or our ethnic background and traditions. No other immigrant group before us has done so. But as others have done, we will not require that government policies be enacted to prefer our particular group.

The voice of the Hispanic community now needs to be heard on this subject. It needs to be heard in order to reassure the rest of the nation that Hispanics are not seeking any special privileges or rights, but only the rights and privileges that belong to ordinary Americans.

There is a reservoir of goodwill on the part of the American public evident in the debate about legislation that has taken place. There is no outcry calling for mass deportation of 11 or 12 million people. There is no real support for criminalizing all illegal immigrants. There is true understanding that the reason for crossing the borders without authority is founded on the need to find a job in order to provide for a livelihood and for the needs of a family. This goodwill is there to be tapped, but it must be reinvigorated by a loud commitment on the part of the Hispanic community that the fundamental principle of the American Idea of "one nation, one standard" will be upheld by the new immigrants as it was by all who came before. The burden is now on the Hispanic community to state unequivocally that they support this fundamental principle.

Acknowledgments

I WISH TO THANK Lawrence Mone, president of the Manhattan Institute for Policy Research, who first encouraged me to write this book and who provided me with the support and assistance of Mark Riebling, the institute's editorial director, and Sam Munson, an associate editor. Many thanks to Deroy Murdock, who edited the original manuscript and provided invaluable assistance. My thanks also go to Dr. Peter Salins, provost of the State University of New York, whose ideas about assimilation are incorporated in much of the book. My friend and former press secretary James Vlasto carefully reviewed every page and remembered some details even better than I did, for which I am grateful. I was lucky to have Bernadette Malone, my editor at the Penguin Group, cheering me along every step of the way. Finally, my secretary, Margarita Ramos Schreiber, deserves an award for her infinite patience in typing and retyping changing versions from an indecipherable manuscript.

Notes

2. Beyond the Mountains

1. "Who's Here: Herman Badillo, Chairman, CUNY," *Dan's Papers* (Long Island), Oct. 15, 1999, pp. 25–26.
2. Badillo, "A Turning Point in My Life," unpublished.
3. "Who's Here."
4. Tamar Jacoby, *Reinventing the Melting Pot* (New York: Basic Books, 2004).
5. Soo Kim Abboud and Jane Y. Kim, *Top of the Class: How Asian Parents Raise High Achievers—and How You Can Too* (New York: Berkley, 2005).

3. The Five-Century Siesta

1. Juan Gonzalez, *Harvest of Empire: A History of Latinos in America* (New York: Viking, 2000).
2. Elizabeth de Lima-Dantas, "Historical Setting," in *Mexico: A Country Study* (Washington, D.C.: United States Government, 1985).
3. Nicholas Lemann, "The Other Underclass: Puerto Ricans in the U.S.," *Atlantic Monthly,* Dec. 1991, p. 96ff.

4. Nathan Glazer and Daniel Patrick Moynihan, *Beyond the Melting Pot: The Negroes, Puerto Ricans, Jews, Italians, and Irish of New York City,* 2nd ed. (Cambridge, Mass.: MIT Press, 1970).
5. Jill Jonnes, *We're Still Here: The Rise, Fall, and Resurrection of the South Bronx* (Boston: Atlantic Monthly Press, 1986).
6. Lemann, "The Other Underclass."

4. The Politics of Education

1. Michael Tomasky, "Identity Politics in New York City: The Tawdry Mosaic," *Nation,* June 21, 1993, p. 860ff.

6. Social Promotion and Other Implements of Ignorance

1. John Leo, "A University's Sad Decline," *U.S. News & World Report,* Aug. 15, 1994.
2. *Washington Post*, June 26, 1998.
3. *New York Post*, Sept. 29, 1999.
4. *New York Times*, Oct. 5, 1994, p. B1.
5. Liz Trotta, "Crumbling NYC Schools Are Giuliani's Latest Monster," *Washington Times,* April 23, 1994, p. A3.
6. James Barron, "Cortines Says He's Quitting," *New York Times,* June 16, 1995, p. A1.
7. *New York Post*, Sept. 19, 1999.

7. The Harvard of the Poor

1. *Amsterdam News*, March 4, 1998.
2. Karen W. Arenson, "Poking Education's Sore Spot," *New York Times,* Jan. 31, 1998.

3. Ibid.

4. James Traub, *City on a Hill: Testing the American Dream at City College* (Reading, Mass.: Addison-Wesley, 1994).

5. Heather MacDonald, "Downward Mobility: The Failure of Open Admissions at City University," *City Journal*, vol. 4, no. 3 (Summer 1994), pp. 10–20.

6. Ibid.

7. Ibid.

8. John Leo, "A University's Sad Decline," *U.S. News & World Report*, Aug. 15, 1994.

9. MacDonald, "Downward Mobility."

10. Jim Sleeper, "City College Faculty Is Wrong to Demand Badillo Resign," *New York Daily News*, April 20, 1995, p. 45.

11. Ibid.

12. Ibid.

13. *Chronicle of Higher Education*, June 5, 1998.

14. *New York Times*, June 6, 1999.

15. Liz Trotta, "Battle Lines Drawn Over Remedial Education; CUNY Standards Boost Activists' Ire," *Washington Times*, June 1, 1998.

16. *Chronicle of Higher Education*, June 5, 1998.

17. Karen W. Arenson, "CUNY to Tighten Admissions Policy at 4-Year Schools," *New York Times*, May 27, 1998, p. A1.

18. *Amsterdam News*, June 3, 1998.

19. *New York Times*, May 27, 1998.

20. *New York Times*, June 6, 1999.

21. *Chronicle of Higher Education*, June 11, 1999.

8. From Kennedy Democrat to Giuliani Republican

1. Michael Tomasky, "Identity Politics in New York City: The Tawdry Mosiac," *Nation*, June 21, 1993.

9. Toward a Unified Culture

1. *New York Post,* March 23, 2006.
2. David Brooks, "Immigrants to Be Proud of," *New York Times,* March 30, 2006.

10. The Hispanic Community in the United States and Latin America: The Next Fifty Years

1. *New York Times,* March 30, 2006.
2. Vicente Fox, "Dreams, Challenges and Threats," Center for U.S.-Mexico Studies, the University of Texas at Dallas, 1998, p. 172.
3. *Judicial Corruption in Developing Countries: Its Causes and Economic Consequences* (Palo Alto: Hoover Institution, Stanford University, 1999).
4. William Ratliff, *Doing It Wrong and Doing It Right* (Palo Alto: Hoover Institution, Stanford University, 2003).

11. One Nation, One Standard

1. Peter D. Salins, *Assimilation, American Style* (New York: Basic Books, 1996).
2. Arthur M. Schlesinger Jr., *The Disuniting of America* (New York: W. W. Norton, 1992).

Index

Abboud, Soo Kim, 29
Adler, Norman, 157
affirmative action, 132, 209
African-Americans, 45
  black studies departments and, 118
  civil rights and, 18–19
  Crown Heights riots and, 152–54
  CUNY enrollment rates for, 6, 110
  division between Puerto Ricans and,
    19–21
  high-school dropout rate among, 28,
    53, 97
  pitching school reform to, 79, 80
  racial divide and, 15–16
  segregation and, 18–19
  see also minority communities, U.S.
Alter, Susan, 166
American Civil Liberties Union, 105
American Jewish Congress, 131
Amsterdam News, 132
Anker, Irving, 78
Antonetti, Evelina, 58
Aparicio, Ariel, 185–87
Asia, economic and educational
    development of, 201–2
Asian-American Legal Defense Fund,
    131
Asian community, 24, 64, 68–69
  education and, 25, 27–29, 32
  "secrets" to success of, 29–30
Aspira, 70, 210

*Aspira of New York, Inc. v. Board of
    Education of the City of New York,* 70
assimilation and acculturation, 1, 3, 44,
    51, 184–89
  civic unity as premise of, 208–9, 213
  cultural unity as premise of, 208
  English language as mechanism of,
    208, 212–13
  Hispanic resistance to, 1, 3, 4, 6–7,
    212
  historical basis of, 207–10
  of illegal immigrants, 206–7, 208–9,
    210
  keys to, 7, 195, 208–10
  multiculturalism vs., 209–13

Badillo, Herman:
  bilingual education advocated in
    Congress by, 57–63
  as Bronx borough president, 23, 97,
    149
  as chair of CUNY board of trustees,
    133–38
  childhood and youth of, 9–15, 20–21,
    57–58, 60, 97
  in city comptroller race, 162, 166–69
  in Congress, 2, 4, 23, 57–63, 189,
    195, 197
  as CUNY student, 15, 30, 111
  as CUNY trustee, 5–6, 23, 24, 109,
    117–38

as deputy mayor, 23, 78, 151, 164, 195

Educational Gates program of, 78–81

educational views and efforts of, *see* education; *specific educational practices*

education of, 12–15, 30, 49–50, 57–58, 96–97

emigration of, 3, 9

English learned by, 12–13, 58, 60

Giuliani's alliance with, 81–88, 157–69, 171, 173, 175

Hispanic vote delivered by, 144–49, 162, 169

as housing relocation commissioner, 23, 25–26, 31, 149

and JFK's presidential campaign, 144–49

law practice of, 22, 58, 139–41

mayoral runs of, 23, 88–90, 136, 150

political involvement and career of, 22–24, 58, 141–49, 149–50, 151, 157–69

racism encountered in youth of, 20–21, 177, 179

religious background of, 10–11

Republican Party supported by, 23–24, 133, 166–67, 174

in vocational programs, 14–15, 49–50, 96–97

Baker, Russell, 151

Balaguer, Joaquin, 39

Barron, James, 86

Baruch College, *see* CUNY

Beame, Abe, 6, 149–50

Beyond the Melting Pot (Glazer and Moynihan), 45

Biaggi, Mario, 158

bilingual education, 2, 4, 57–71, 107, 122, 208, 212

attempted elimination of, 66–70

congressional debate and legislation on, 57–63

among Cuban community in Dade County, 60–61

immersion programs and, 67, 69–70

measuring results of, 67

opposition to, 64

bilingualism, 70, 208

as monolingualism, 4, 65–66

bilingual voting, 2, 26, 208, 212

Bloomberg, Michael, 88–91

Board of Education, NYC, 88, 89, 161, 167

bilingual education programs reexamined by, 65

budget of, 81, 82–86

financial audit of, 83–86

1960s decentralization plan of, 52–54

special education budget of, 101–2

structure of, 81–82, 97

Board of Elections, NYC, 22, 26, 143, 148–49

Board of Regents, N.Y., 134–35

border security, 192, 196–97, 205–6, 211–12

Bowker, Albert, 113

Brady, Jacqueline V., 125

Bratton, William, 169–70, 171

Bronx, 23, 97, 122, 149

see also South Bronx

Bronx High School of Science, 28

Brooklyn College, *see* CUNY

Brooklyn Law School, 15, 22, 50

Brooks, David, 187–88

Bruno, Joseph, 135

Burgos, Tonio, 151

Buscaglia, Eduardo, 199–200

Bush, George W., 192–93, 205–6

Caguas, P.R., 9, 17

California, 35, 193

bilingual education in, 66–69

dropout rates in, 66–67

educational reorganization in, 107–8, 132

educational standards implemented in, 106

Hispanic population of, 43

Callaghan, Alice, 66

Cambridge Rindge and Latin School, 105

Caribbean Basin Initiative, 7, 202

Caribe Democratic Club, 142–43

Castro, Fidel, 39, 60, 194

Catholic Church, Catholicism, 11, 17–18, 19, 36

Census, U.S., of 2000, 43

Census Bureau, U.S., 179–80, 184, 186

Center for Educational Innovation, 85

Central American Free Trade Agreement, 202

charter schools, 54

Chavez, Linda, 184–85, 210, 211

Chisholm, Shirley, 79, 111, 113

Cisneros, Henry, 168

City College, *see* CUNY

City on a Hill, The (Traub), 112

City University of New York, *see* CUNY

City University of New York, The: An Institution Adrift (task force report), 126–31

Civil Rights Act of 1964, 18–19, 131

Class (Fussell), 137

College Discovery program, 182–83

colleges and universities, 30
  educational politics at, 5–6
  minority demographics of, 6, 16, 27, 50, 110, 113, 114, 117, 137, 181

Columbia High School, 92–93

Columbus, Christopher, 35, 36, 38

COMP-STAT, 169

Congress, U.S., 19, 26, 78
  Badillo in, 2, 4, 23, 57–63, 189, 195, 197
  immigration and border security issue in, 192, 205–6, 211–12
  special education protections enacted by, 101, 102
  see also House of Representative, U.S.; Senate, U.S.

Congressional Black Caucus, 80

Connerly, Ward, 80

Co-op City, 46

Coopers & Lybrand, 83–84

Cortines, Ramon, 82–83, 86, 107

Crew, Rudolph, 86–88

crime, 150
  poverty linked to, 159–60
  reduction under Giuliani of, 6, 87–88, 159–60, 163–64, 169–70, 171–73
  U.S.-Latin cooperation on, 202–3

Crouch, Stanley, 172

Crown Heights riots, 6, 23, 152–54, 156

Cuban community, 43
  bilingual education programs in, 60–61
  Republican support from, 194

CUNY (City University of New York), 15, 23, 24, 30, 49, 108, 109–38, 161, 167
  Badillo as student at, 15, 30, 111
  Badillo as trustee of, 5–6, 23, 24, 109, 117–38
  budget of, 115, 116, 117
  City College's reputation and, 110–11
  Giuliani task force's examination of, 124–31
  honors program at, 135–36
  Hostos assessment-test scandal and, 122–24
  Jeffries uproar at, 118–19, 121
  open admissions at, *see* open admissions at CUNY
  Puerto Rican police training and, 202–3
  remediation at, *see* remediation at CUNY
  standards and testing adopted and implemented at, 130–33, 134, 135, 181
  student demographics of, 6, 16, 110, 113, 114, 116, 117, 137–38, 181
  student strike at, 5, 74, 109–10, 113, 136

Cuomo, Mario, 23, 83, 109, 166

de Lima-Dantas, Elizabeth, 38

de Luca, Geraldine, 120

Democratic Party, 168
  Badillo as critic of, 167, 174–75
  Badillo's final split with, 166–67, 174
  constituents taken for granted by, 174–75, 193
  internal conflict and factions of, 142, 144, 147–48, 150, 156–57
  NYC clubs of, 141–42, 143–44, 145
  and shift in Hispanic vote, 192–94

De Sapio, Carmine, 143

Dinkins, David, 6, 23, 80–81, 86, 160, 167, 168
  Crown Heights as failure of, 152–54, 156
  as divisive force, 153–54, 155–57
  minority support for, 162
  NYC mismanaged by, 151–58, 165

Disuniting of America, The (Schlesinger), 209
Dominican community, 43, 47–48
Douglas, William O., 68–69
"dual language" approach, 70–71

Edelstein, Julius CC, 113
education, 3, 4–6
bilingual, *see* bilingual education
"dual language" approach to, 70–71
as gateway to success in U.S., 4, 138, 195
Hispanic community's attitude toward, 3, 4–5, 27, 30–32, 50, 195–96
as important tool for immigrant groups, 24, 27–32, 195
in Latin America, 40–41
politics of, 3–4, 49–55, 76–77, 109, 113–14, 134–35
school decentralization plans and, 52–54
segregation and, 18–19
teacher strikes and, 53
value of, 25, 27–29, 32, 137
va y ven syndrome and, 44–45
see also school system, NYC
educational establishment:
academic standards and testing opposed from within, 119, 122–23
leftist ideology of, 120–21
minorities failed by, 4–5, 44, 48, 49–50, 54, 103, 195–96
minority enfranchisement by, 118, 119–21, 136–37
racial politics of, 76–77
value of education cheapened by, 137
Educational Gates program, 78–81
elections, U.S.:
of 1960, 144–49
of 2004, 3, 192
Elementary and Secondary Education Act (ESEA), 59, 62–63
Elion, Gertrude, 111
Elwell, John, 85–86
English language:
Badillo's learning of, 12–13, 58, 60
cultural unity and, 208, 212–13
Hispanic community and, 4, 212

ethnic federalism, 209
ethnic groups, *see* immigrant groups

FairTest, 105
Falcon, Angelo, 47
Fernandez, Dolores, 124
Ferrini-Mundy, Joan, 106
feudalism, 37–38
Fichtner, Paula, 137
Figueroa, Juan, 132
Fink, Stanley, 119
Florida, 35, 43, 104
Fox, Vicente, 198
Frankfurter, Felix, 111
Franks, Gary, 79–80
Friedman, Stanley, 158
Fussell, Paul, 137

Garth, David, 158
GI Bill, 137
"gifted children" programs, 99–101
Giuliani, Rudolph W., vii–x, 6, 23–24, 55, 65, 89, 133, 175
crime reduction and, 6, 87–88, 159–60, 163–64, 169–70, 171–73
CUNY task force appointed by, 124–25
education policies and reforms of, 81–88, 118, 122, 124–28, 131, 132–33, 164
mayoral campaigns of, 151, 157–69
minority support for, 162–63, 169, 170
policing philosophy and policy of, 87–88, 159–60, 169–70, 172–73
Glazer, Nathan, 45
Goldstein, Matthew, 134
grade inflation, 123–24
Greek community, 64, 189–90
Green, Mark, 89
Guzman, Sandra, 185–87

Haaren High School, 14–15, 49, 96–98
Harding, Raymond B., 157, 158
Harriman, Averell, 143
Harvest of Empire (Gonzalez), 38
Herbert, Bob, 132–33
High School for Marine and Aviation Trades, 97, 98–99

Hispanic culture:
  lack of racial divide in, 16–17, 22, 37, 179
  religion and, 17–18, 19, 36
  roots of, 32–33
  Spanish colonialism at root of, 35–42
Hispanics, Hispanic community:
  assimilation and acculturation resisted by, 1, 3, 4, 6–7, 212
  attitude toward education among, 3, 4–5, 27, 30–32, 50, 195–96
  criticism of Badillo's party switch from, 166–67
  discrimination toward, 7, 196
  as entrepreneurs, 184–87, 194
  failed by educational system, 4–5, 44, 48, 49–50, 54, 195–96
  failure to adjust to life in U.S. by, 27
  failure to learn English, 4, 212
  high-school dropout rate among, 1, 28, 30, 51, 53, 66–67, 97
  as immigrants, 1, 3, 7, 42–43, 47–48, 184–88
  independence from social welfare needed for, 3, 8, 50–51, 54, 103, 183
  lack of racial divide among, 16–17, 25, 179
  as largest U.S. minority, 43, 191
  in migration to U.S., 1, 3
  as part of unified U.S. culture, 183–84
  pitching school reform to, 79
  police relations with, 170
  political influence of, 26–27, 43–44, 191–94
  political party shift among, 192–94
  reading habits of, 30–31
  reasons for migration to U.S. of, 3, 7, 189, 197–98, 203–4, 213
  self-identification of, 180
  self-segregation by, 7, 196
  talents and capabilities of, 183–84
  in 2000 census, 43
  as underachievers, 2, 3, 195–96
  see also minority communities, U.S.
Hmong, 28
Hostos Community College, 122–24
House of Representatives, U.S., 62, 78, 192, 206

Education and Labor Committee of, 59, 61–62, 78
  Judiciary Committee of, 26
  see also Congress, U.S.
housing, 2, 194, 195
  Badillo as NYC commissioner of housing relocation, 23, 25–26, 31, 149
Hunter College, *see* CUNY
Huxtable, Ada Louise, 111

illegal immigration, 7, 47–48, 184, 196–97, 205
  congressional debate and legislation on, 192, 205–6, 211–12
  over Mexican border, 197–98, 205–6
  as national debate, 211–12
  saturation media coverage of, 205–6, 211–12
immersion programs, 67, 69–70
immigrant groups, 3
  adjustment to life in the U.S. by, 24–32, 184–88
  cultural identity of, 25, 189
  education as important tool for, 24, 27–32, 195
  response to challenge of adjustment by differing, 24–25, 27–28
  rights and rights demonstrations of, 188–89, 209
  see also Hispanics, Hispanic community; minority communities, U.S.
immigration, 1, 3, 42–43, 197–98, 205–6, 211–12
  causes of, 3, 7, 189, 197–98, 203–4, 213
  see also border security; illegal immigration
Institute for Puerto Rican Policy, 47
Inter-American Development Bank, 202
Italian-Americans, community and tradition valued highly by, 25

Jeffries, Leonard, 118–19, 121
Jerro, Andrew, 186
Jewish community:
  and Crown Heights riots, 152–54
  education valued highly by, 27, 32

job market, 2, 45, 47, 164, 172
John Jay College of Criminal Justice, *see* CUNY
Johnson, Lyndon, 19, 193–94
Jonnes, Jill, 45–46

Keith (school friend), 20–21, 179
Kelling, George, 159
Kennedy, Edward, 61
Kennedy, Jacqueline "Jackie," 146–47
Kennedy, John F., 22, 143–49
    Badillo in 1960 campaign of, 144–49
    minority support for, 146, 193, 194
Kennedy, Robert F., 144
Kim, Jane, 29
Kimmick, Christopher, 124
King, Martin Luther, Jr., 19
Klein, Joel, 89
Koch, Ed, 23, 78, 79, 81, 150–51, 164

La Guardia, Fiorello, 146, 166
Latin America, 199–202
    culture of, *see* Hispanic culture
    education in, 40–41
    political polling in, 41–42
    poverty in, 7, 42
    social and political structure of, 39–42, 198–99
Latin Americans, *see* Hispanics, Hispanic community
Lau v. Nichols, 68–70
Lee, Peggy, 14
Lemann, Nicholas, 44–45, 46–47
Levin, Jake, 104–5
Levy, Harold O., 88
Liberal Party, 157, 158, 166
Lindsay, John, 23, 110, 113, 149, 173
literacy tests, voting rights and, 25–26, 147
Lockheed Martin, 12
Los Angeles Unified School District, 107–8
Lurie, Ellen, 58
Lynch, Bill, 151
Lynch, Gerald W., 202

Macchiarola, Frank, 79, 80
McCoy, Rhody, 52–53
MacDonald, Heather, 125

Mafia, 158, 172–73
Manes, Donald, 150
Manhattan Institute, 7, 85, 105, 159, 210
Manhattanville Junior High School, 20–21
Maple, Jack, 169
Marcantonio, Vito, 146
Massachusetts, standardized testing in, 104
Melgarejo, Liliana, 188–89
Mendez, Isabel, 142
Mendez, Tony, 142–43
Merli, John, 145
Mexican American Legal Defense and Educational Fund, 64, 210
Mexican Free Trade Agreement, 202
Mexico, immigration to U.S. from, 43, 197–98, 205–6, 211–12
minority communities, U.S.:
    cultural identity of, 25, 189, 209–13
    in CUNY student population, 110, 113, 114, 116, 117, 137–38
    demographics of, in higher education, 6, 16, 27, 50, 110, 113, 114, 117, 137–38, 181
    education and standards as key to progress for, 138, 195
    failed by educational establishment, 4–5, 44, 48, 49–50, 54, 103, 195–96
    and 1960 presidential campaign, 144–49
    NYC high-school dropout rates of, 1, 28, 30, 51, 53, 97
    voter eligibility and participation of, 3, 22, 27, 43–44, 147–49, 162–63, 169, 170, 191–94
    see also immigrant groups; *specific minorities*
Monument Mountain Regional High School, 104–5
Morning, John, 129
Moses, Yolanda, 120
Moynihan, Daniel Patrick, 45, 111
mulattoes (*morenos*), 37
multiculturalism, 209–13
    of NYC, 177–78, 189–90
Muñoz Marín, Luis, 203

NAACP Legal Defense Fund, 131
Nation, 54–55
National Council of La Raza, 210
National Council of Teachers, 106
Nelson, Lemrick, 152–53
New York, N.Y.:
    Board of Education in, *see* Board of
        Education, NYC
    budgetary state of, 164–65
    crime rate in, 150, 153, 169, 171–73
    decline of, under Koch, 150–51
    Democratic clubs in, 141–42, 143–44,
        145
    demographics of, 74, 177–78
    deterioration of city services in,
        150–51, 163–65
    Dinkins's mismanagement of, 151–58
    duplication of government agencies in,
        164–65
    garbage collection in, 172–73
    Giuliani's crime reduction plans for, 6,
        87–88, 159–60, 163–64, 169–70,
        171–73
    governability of, 163–65, 173, 174
    immigrant rights demonstration in,
        188–89
    job market in, 164, 172
    multiculturalism of, 177–78, 189–90
    as racially divided city, 19–21
    school system, *see* school system, NYC
    welfare rolls in, 155, 160–61, 170
    voting rights in, 25–26
New York City Marathon, 178
New York Civil Liberties Union, 157
New York Daily News, 122
New York Jets, 151
New York Post, 90–91, 155, 185–87
New York State:
    university systems in, *see* CUNY;
        SUNY
New York Times, 92–93, 132–33, 172,
    188–89
Nixon, Richard, 149
Nuñez, Emilio, 139, 141, 142

Ocean Hill–Brownsville School District,
    52–54
Ohrenstein, Manfred, 125
Opara, Ugoshi, 93

open admissions at CUNY, 5–6
    Badillo's opposition and efforts to
        reverse, 114, 118, 167
    critics of, 110, 113–14, 118
    elimination of, 134–35
    implementation of, 110–17
    supporters of, 114–15, 137
    task force recommendation on reversal
        of, 127–28
    unintended consequences of, 116
Operation Bootstrap, 2, 203
Organization of American States, 202
Ortiz, Rose, 116
Out of the Barrio (Chavez), 211

Paolucci, Anne A., 121–22, 129, 133
Pataki, George, 55, 89, 121–22, 133
Paterson, Basil, 168
Paz, Octavio, 200
Perkins, Carl, 62
poverty, 159–60
    in Latin America, 7, 42
    in U.S., 1, 45, 180–81, 194
Powers, Peter, 158
Proposition 209, 132
Proposition 277, 66–68
Protestantism, 10–11, 18, 194
Puerto Rican Legal Defense Fund, 131, 210
Puerto Ricans, Puerto Rican community,
    24, 26
    division between African-Americans
        and, 19–21
    family structure among, 45, 47, 48
    racial divide and, 16–17, 19
    refusal to give up Spanish by, 61
    unemployment among, 45, 47
    va y ven syndrome among, 44–45
    see also Hispanics, Hispanic community
Puerto Rico, 9–11, 39, 202–3
    educational system in, 19, 26
    population of, 43
    religious life in, 10–11, 17–18

Queens College, *see* CUNY
Quie, Albert, 61

racial divide, 15–22
    among Hispanics, 16–17
    in U.S., 15–16, 18–22, 37, 178–80

racial profiling, 173
Ramirez, Roberto, 175
Randolph, A. Philip, 111
Rangel, Charles, 132, 168
Ratliff, William, 200–201
Ravitch, Diane, 99–100
Regents Diploma, 54
Regular Democratic Organization
    (RDO), 143–44, 145, 147–48
remediation at CUNY, 112–17, 130–32
    Badillo resolution on limiting, 128–31
    euphemisms for, 124
    Giuliani task force's examination of,
        124–31
    growth and extent of, 115–16, 126
    limitations placed on, 135
    program funding for, 115
    spending on, 115, 116, 117, 126
Republican Party, 158, 166
    Badillo's switch to, 23–24, 133,
        166–67, 174
    and shift in Hispanic vote, 192–94
Reyes, Luis O., 65
Riordan, Richard, 170
Roberts, Richard T., 125
Rockefeller, Nelson, 150
Roosevelt, Eleanor, 146
Roosevelt, Franklin, 193
Rosenbaum, Yankel, 152–53
Rosenthal, A. M., 111
Rosetti, Frank, 145
Rosselló González, Pedro, 202

Salk, Jonas, 111
Santangelo, Alfred E., 145
Santiago, Isaura, 123
Schlesinger, Arthur M., Jr., 209, 210
Schmidt, Benno C., Jr., 125, 133
school decentralization, 52–54
school system, NYC:
    bilingual education programs in,
        63–66, 68, 70
    Bloomberg's control of, 89–91
    corruption and cronyism in, 81–82
    Educational Gates program in,
        78–81
    Giuliani's policies and reforms of,
        81–88, 118, 122, 124–28, 131,
        132–33, 164

graduates unprepared for college after,
    111–12, 113, 126, 181
minority dropout rates in, 1, 28, 30,
    51, 53, 97
segregated classes in, 91–99
social promotion in, 73, 74, 77–81
special education spending in, 84,
    101–2
spending per student in, 84–85,
    101–2
student demographics of, 74, 77
success of Asian students within,
    28–29
see also Board of Education, NYC;
    education; *specific schools*
school vouchers, 54
Schwartz, Richard, 125
SEEK (Search for Education, Elevation
    and Knowledge), 113, 181–83
Segarra, Ninfa, 171
segregation, school, 18–19, 91–99
Senate, U.S., 61–62, 192, 206
    see also Congress, U.S.
September 11, 2001, terrorist attacks of,
    175, 178
Shanker, Albert, 52–53
Siegel, Norman, 157
Silver, Sheldon, 135
Simon, Stanley, 150
Simonetti, Angelo, 141–42
60 Minutes, 80
slavery, 18, 19
Smith, Jean Kennedy, 143
Smith, Steve, 143, 144
social promotion, 4, 5, 73–91, 161,
    167
    elimination from NYC schools of,
        90–91
    fear and guilt at root of, 73, 74, 76–77
    racist philosophy in, 75–76
    as unacceptable to Badillo, 77–78,
        167
social welfare services, 181–83, 195
    Hispanic independence from, 3, 8,
        50–51, 54, 103, 183
    removing racist labels from, 183
    see also welfare
South Bronx, 47, 78
    burning of, 23, 45–46

Spanish Empire, 3
    commercial goals of, 37–38
    racial mixing in, 36–37
    at root of Hispanic culture, 35–42,
        200–201
special education programs, 5, 101–3
    as dead end for students, 102–3
    spending on, 84, 101–2, 103
    student placement in, 102–3
standards and standardized testing, 87,
        90–91, 104–6, 161, 167
    CUNY adoption and implementation
        of, 127–28, 130–33, 134, 135, 181
    opposition to, 104–5, 119, 122–23,
        131–33
Stone, Richard, 131
Stuyvesant High School, 28
Sullivan, Edward C., 130
SUNY (State University of New York), 127
Supreme Court, U.S., 68–69
Sutton, Percy, 168

teachers' union, 4, 52–53, 54, 70, 80
Texas, 35, 43, 107
Thernstrom, Abigail, 105, 210
Thernstrom, Stephan, 210
Thomas, Clarence, 79
Tomasky, Michael, 54–55, 154
Top of the Class (Abboud and Kim), 29
tracking, academic, 4, 5, 91–99
    vocational programs and, 93, 95–99
Traub, James, 112

United Nations, 41
    Economic Commission for Latin
        America and the Caribbean of, 202
United States, 1, 3, 51, 184–89, 202
    education and standards as gateways
        to success in, 4, 138, 195
    Hispanic-owned businesses in,
        184–87, 194
    immigrant groups in, *see* immigrant
        groups; *specific groups*

immigration to, *see* illegal
        immigration; immigration
    as land of opportunity, 42–43, 44
    poverty in, 1, 45, 180–81, 194
    Protestantism in, 18, 194
    as racially divided culture, 15–16,
        18–22, 37, 178–80
Unz, Ron, 66

Vargas, Daniel, 41
va y ven syndrome, 44–45
Village Voice, 86
vocational programs:
    Badillo as student in, 14–15, 49–50,
        96–97
    as form of tracking, 93, 95–99
    outdated materials and curriculum in,
        97–99
    students unprepared after, 96
voting, voter participation:
    bilingual, 2, 26, 208
    literacy tests as hurdle in, 25–26,
        147
    of minority communities, 3, 22, 27,
        43–44, 147–49, 162–63, 169, 170,
        191–94, 213
    and registration for 1960 presidential
        campaign, 147–49
Voting Rights Act (1965), 25–26

Wade, Richard, 132
Wagner, Robert F., 23, 149
Wallace, Mike, 80
Washington Heights, 47, 154
Watts, J. F., 120
welfare, in NYC, 155, 160–61, 170
    see also social welfare services
We're Still Here (Jonnes), 45–46
Wilson, John Q., 159
Wilson, Pete, 193
World War II, 42, 203

Zhou, Min, 27–28